This powerful book is certain to change the lives of countless people, and we couldn't be more thrilled that it is now available to the public. Yvonne Grant's practical, biblically grounded steps for overcoming addiction, spiritual oppression, emotional issues, and many other kinds of affliction are based on her own personal experience. She now travels the world sharing the knowledge and wisdom God has given her to speak to others who are looking for genuine freedom from bondage. My wife, Kelli, and I give this book our highest recommendation.

—*Pastor Dan and Kelli Hamann*
Canyon Creek Church, North Everett Campus

TRANSFORMED

Keys for Your
Supernatural
Journey
to Freedom

TRANSFORMED

*Keys for Your
Supernatural
Journey
to Freedom*

YVONNE GRANT

Published by Redemption Press, PO Box 427, Enumclaw, WA 98022
Toll Free (844) 2REDEEM (273-3336)

Redemption Press is honored to present this title in partnership with the author. The views expressed or implied in this work are those of the author. Redemption Press provides our imprint seal representing design excellence, creative content, and high-quality production.

ISBN: 978-1-68314-806-7 (Paperback)
ePub: 978-1-68314-808-1
Mobi: 978-1-68314-807-4

LCCN: 2018965758

To my Lord and Savior Jesus Christ,
this book is your story.
One that reveals your fierce relentless love,
your unfailing forgiveness, your grace and mercy.
You transformed me and my life,
and I love you!

To my family who sacrificed so much for me.
You gave me the time that
I needed to complete the work,
and your sacrifice did not go unnoticed.
I love you beyond words
and thank God every day for each of you.

ACKNOWLEDGEMENTS

I'm so incredibly grateful to everyone who so generously invested in the success of *Transformed*. I love you dearly and pray the Lord Jesus richly bless you and cause you to prosper in all good things!

I would like to extend a very special thank you to:

Geoffrey and Janell Gilmore, Joe and Lisa Leonardi, Tony and Linda Morehouse, Earl and Charlene Johnsen, Josiah and Karlee Blake, Pete and Stacey Michel, Dan and Kelli Hamann.

Thank you for working so selflessly beside me! Your participation, your gifts, talents and treasures have made *Transformed* a reality! I'm forever grateful!

TABLE OF CONTENTS

Chapter 1: Supernatural Encounters...13

Chapter 2: The Internal Conflict 27

Chapter 3: Spirit Realm Revealed 37

Chapter 4: The Gospel 53

Chapter 5: Holy Spirit Introductions 65

Chapter 6: Hearing His Voice 85

Chapter 7: Faith 105

Chapter 8: Intimacy with God 121

Chapter 9: Yielded 135

Chapter 10: Trials, Transitions, and Changes...............................163

Chapter 11: Created for Purpose 189

Chapter 12: Preparation of a Warrior: Part 1 209

Chapter 13: Preparation of a Warrior: Part 2 221

Chapter 14: Winning in Warfare: Part 1.......................................237

Chapter 15: Winning in Warfare: Part 2 245

Chapter 16: Conclusion 253

Chapter I
SUPERNATURAL ENCOUNTERS

How long must I wrestle with my thoughts
and day after day have sorrow in my heart?
How long will my enemy triumph over me?
(Psalm 13:2)

A LIFE WITHOUT GOD

I grew up without any knowledge of God. There was no mention of him in the house. Church attendance was not part of my life. I had no understanding of God's reality. Unaware of his presence, I didn't know God has always been and that he existed before the universe was created. I didn't know his desire has always been to have a loving, trusting relationship with me—the kind of relationship that brings about a miraculous and eternal change within.

When I was a little girl, my parents had a band. I remember running around dancing and singing with them in a blue cloud of smoke as they spent hours during the week practicing for their gigs in taverns on the weekends. My weekends were spent with babysitters.

Alcoholism became a prevalent invading part of my parents' lives, and as a result, it affected mine. On many occasions, they returned home in an upheaval of emotion after their gigs. I would lie in bed listening to them yell and argue with one another. Their arguing scared me, yet I was too terrified to get out of bed and make my presence known.

My father had always told me growing up, "I want the very best for you," and he guided me with a firm hand and strict rules. If the rules were broken, the consequence was quick to follow. That made getting out of bed when I was supposed to be asleep out of the question.

Las Vegas, bands, and bars were a backdrop for part of my childhood. Many nights I was placed into other people's care. This opened my young life to the lustful, fleshly deeds of others. Without sharing graphic details, I endured the perils of physical, emotional, mental, and sexual abuse. I was also exposed to the loveless disdain of prejudice, based on the color of my skin, from someone who was bound to me as family.

When I was eleven, my family moved from Nevada to Washington. My father did not believe in God at the time, and he dove further into a quest to find spiritual power. This search led him to seek power in witchcraft and magic. Misguided, he became fascinated with occult practices, and he read books on black magic, witchcraft, and casting spells.

Unusual and mysterious things began happening in the house. The furnace began turning on by itself. The lamps would turn on and off. I heard sounds of creaking doors when everyone else was asleep. Sometimes when these strange things happened, what happened next was just as strange. For example, when the lights would turn on by themselves, my father would open the attic door and yell up, "Gus, turn the lights back off!"—and the lights would turn off!

With this becoming a normal lifestyle for my dad, I was ushered into all sorts of demonic situations in the guise of innocent childhood games. Ouija boards, tarot cards, horoscopes, hypnosis, and transcendental meditation became daily activities for me. This gave the devil a stronghold in my life.

At the age of fifteen, I dropped out of high school, ran away from home, and headed for Portland, Oregon. My hope was to find independence, freedom, and love. That didn't happen. Without any purpose to my days, I drank, smoked, and stayed stoned to avoid the emptiness.

One night I was abruptly awakened as police stormed into my bedroom. Shining a bright light in my face, they began accusing me of stealing firearms. I had no idea what they were talking about. I didn't have any guns. In stern voices, they demanded to know where I put them.

Once cleared of the allegations, I began thinking, Surely this can't be all there is to life. I decided to return home and go back to high school.

Back home and in school, I didn't want to graduate a year behind my classmates. My goal was to complete my junior and senior years in one year. In order to do this, I had to obtain permission from the student counselors and the school board. They were not sure I would be able to accomplish this, but they granted my request.

I had an arduous schedule that year. I took my junior classes during the day and worked on my senior classes at night. At the end of that year, I graduated with my class with a 3.8 GPA. My dream had come true, and I had succeeded in my academic goals. This gave me a sense of stability. Finding acceptance and love from my classmates, I felt I had successfully turned my life around. Life felt very settled and peaceful. Nothing could stand in my way now.

At a party I was having for a few friends, I found myself face-to-face with cocaine. I felt an incredible sense of fear. When my sister asked, "Do you want to try it?" I said, "No way!" Then the guy who had declared his love for me leaned over my shoulder and said, "Go ahead, baby; I would never let you take anything that would hurt you."

Reluctantly, I did it.

It only took ten minutes for the drug to convince me that "This is bliss!" I quickly asked for more. The drug filled me with an increased sense of confidence, joy, and security. I made one simple choice that day, but I didn't realize that one choice would unleash such a destructive force that would change life as I knew it.

With one single snort of cocaine, I entered my own internal prison. I was held captive, chained to a full-fledged addiction that spiraled into the use of other drugs, alcoholism, and the immoral life that went along with it. I had wanted a better life, but instead I found myself plunged into a horrible prison cell of my own making because of my poor decisions.

Eventually I became a small-time drug dealer, a liar, and a thief. I did whatever was necessary to sustain the lifestyle of an addict. This vicious cycle continued for eleven and a half years. No matter how hard I tried to escape, the strong chains that the drugs had crafted would abruptly yank me back into my internal cell. This cycle left me completely bankrupt of any hope for change. With each attempt and failure to escape, the black hole of emptiness grew within me—until one night I encountered an unfamiliar man.

THE FIRST ENCOUNTER

That day in 1988 began like any other summer day. The flower beds were in full bloom, and the air was full of their sweet aroma. A cool, gentle breeze made its way through the house as the open windows allowed the scent to fill the rooms.

But that evening's events would be anything but ordinary.

As twilight approached, I went about my typical routine: dinner, dishes, and getting my five-year-old ready for bed. Then I walked through the house making sure all the windows were closed. Before going to bed, I took about an hour to sit back and relax, basking in some peace and quiet after another full day with my busy five-year-old. Then, completely exhausted, I climbed into bed and quickly fell asleep.

I'm not sure how long I had been asleep, but I was suddenly awakened by a touch on my big toe. I opened my eyes to see a man standing at the side of my bed. I didn't know who he was, but I wasn't startled or afraid, which seemed bizarre to me.

He stood silently, cloaked in a robe that looked like burlap, with a hood that covered his head. Without a single word, he placed his left index finger over his lips to signal me to be silent and not to wake my husband. I instinctively understood and complied.

I looked over at my husband; he was fast asleep. Turning back, I looked at the man who was still standing at my bedside. As I watched, he silently raised his left arm and pointed toward the large picture window in our bedroom. Intuitively, I knew he wanted me to go to the window so he could show me something. Without any questions or feelings of mistrust, I got out of bed and took small steps toward the window to see what he was pointing at.

Though this happened almost thirty years ago, I can still vividly recall the moment that I stepped before him. He stood about two feet from the edge of the bed, giving me just enough room to walk between him and the bed itself.

As I got close to him, I suddenly became aware of a light that emanated from him. The closer I got, the more radiant he appeared. The moment I stepped in front of him, I was enveloped in a luminous white light that exuded from him as if he himself were light. His robe no longer appeared to be burlap. It now looked like it was made from glorious rays of white sunlight, yet I could look upon it without pain from the glare of its brilliance.

As I passed in front of him to get to the window, I felt tremendous warmth that exuded from his very being as it gently touched my left cheek. Standing there, encompassed by the light and warmth of his presence, I felt a tremendous sense of peace inside.

When I looked out the window, I saw a single bright star hanging in the sky that seemed to light up the entire sky by itself. Amazed and curious, I looked at the star and wondered, *What does this all mean?* As I turned to ask the man that question, he was gone.

Where did he go?

Back in bed, I gazed around the room wondering who he was. *What does the star mean? Where did he go?* My thoughts began to fade as I slowly drifted back to sleep.

When I awoke the next morning, I wanted to share my experience. My dad was the first person I saw that day, so I quickly shared my experience with him. I stood in disbelief as he chuckled and said, "See what doing hallucinogenic drugs will do to you?"

I thought, *I will never share this experience with anyone again.*

To this day, it amazes me that while I was awakened from a sound sleep and saw a man I did not know standing at the side of my bed, not knowing where he came from or how he got into the house, nothing in me was afraid of him. How could this be? How was it that I did not freak out, scream, or immediately wake my husband? No matter how many times I revisit that moment, I find nothing but peace.

In the midst of my sin, there was nothing threatening about his presence. As he laid his finger on my big toe, stood at my bedside, and pointed out the window, I was at complete peace. Having this experience attributed to drug use, however, made me choose to put the memory away and never speak of it again. Sadly, the destructive cycle of addiction continued to gain momentum every day.

Though drugs had such a strong hold on me, no one would have ever guessed this was going on behind the closed doors of my home.

The toll of addiction was kept under tight wraps, and a good appearance was everything. Although appearance might have communicated to outsiders that my life was grand, behind closed doors hid the complete opposite.

As others saw things, I was married to my high school sweetheart and we were incredibly happy. Behind closed doors, though, was the devious working of the unceasing grip of addiction that placed a heavy strain on us and our relationship. When the euphoria of the high faded away, we went from being high school sweethearts to champions in the fighting ring. We no longer knew how to relate to each other outside of being high. We had created a great façade on the outside, but we were being devoured on the inside.

In the midst of the addiction, with the fighting and the chaos, I would put on a smile and carry out my daily responsibilities in an attempt to keep most people from finding out about the secret life I was living. The addiction was ugly and ruthless as it held me captive to its calling and cravings for eleven and a half years. Often I would wrestle in my mind, concluding that I didn't want to live like that anymore, and I would set out to change things. Unfortunately, I made the same mistake over and over again as I would foolishly think, I have not used for a month; surely I'm in control. In the foolishness of this mindset, I was deceived into believing that I could do a little bit and be okay.

It only took one time of using again for the addiction to take back the reigns of control. For the next three days, the drugs would force me into a darker place, and I would use enough to make up for the thirty days I had gone without. I would make several failed attempts to escape the snare of addiction—only to find myself back in its destructive hold.

Every effort to get free from the addiction only led to an increase in use. An insatiable desire demanded payment, and dealing drugs became a necessity for me to maintain the addiction. Stealing quickly became another devious way to meet the requirement of my own desire for the drug.

Years passed by as I wrestled with my thoughts, creating an internal frustration. I desired to escape this life of addiction but could not overcome the seduction of euphoria, no matter how temporary it was. With more failed attempts to escape the vicious cycle of destruction, my lying, cheating, and stealing continued so that the incessant craving could be fully satisfied as I got high for the day.

SECOND ENCOUNTER

In October 1992, I planned a special weekend for my tenth wedding anniversary by organizing a three-day drug fest. To be honest, this really was no different than any other weekend, except there was a special reason to celebrate. To ensure that our ravenous appetites would be fully satisfied, I stocked up in advance, making sure that the drug supply would not run out. Little did I know that my experiences after this particular celebration would change the course of my life.

Filled with anticipation, I decided not to wait for Friday, but we began our celebration that Thursday evening. We continued through Saturday night without a care in the world. I was with the love of my life, and in our minds we were having a great time together. It is only now that I can clearly see the deception of the drug. It gives the user an empty promise of a euphoric life, lasting as long as the drug's effect.

At the end of our three-day celebration, I woke up Sunday afternoon crying from an excruciating pain down deep in my belly. As I was writhing in bed, I thought, *I'm dreaming!* As I wiped the tears away, I looked at my hands and realized that I was awake. This intense pain that seemed to be coming from the very center of my being could not be ignored or dismissed. Cradling my stomach, I frantically asked myself, "Why am I crying? What is this pain I feel deep inside me?"

Suddenly I heard a voice from the side of my bed! I turned to my right, fully expecting to see someone there, but I saw no one. Turning to my left, I looked at my husband, who was peacefully sleeping next to me. Settling back in the bed and staring at the ceiling, I heard the voice again, saying, "You have been calling me. Here I am! Now what are you going to do?"

At that question, I turned again toward the voice. To my surprise, I saw that man—the same man who had come to me before and stood at my bedside. This time he was kneeling on one knee at the side of my bed. Without any fear, I just laid there staring at him. There was something very different about him in this second encounter. I thought it was very odd that I could see him, yet I could also see right through him as if he were a ghost.

I now understand this experience to be "seeing in the spirit." When I ponder this event, it leads me to ask, "How was I able to see the Lord with my eyes if at that time I was spiritually dead to God?" This is still a mystery to me that offers no other explanation than to say, "It was simply the goodness and grace of God!" Regardless of my inability to understand, this one thing I knew for sure: he was definitely the same man who had appeared to me three and a half years earlier. This man, whom I still did not know personally, had indeed come to visit me a second time.

As I was looking at him, he placed his elbow on the bed, gently curling up his fingers into a fist as he tucked them up under his chin. He looked me straight in the eyes and asked again, "What are you going to do?" Immediately I began to wrestle with this question, asking myself over and over again, "What am I going to do?"

I knew exactly what he was asking. Somehow I clearly understood the unspoken question that was being asked: "Will you choose a life with me, or will you continue to choose your life of addiction?" How I answered this question would determine the course of my life.

Psalm 107:13–14 says it like this: "Then they cried to the LORD in their trouble, and he saved them from their distress. He brought them out of darkness, the utter darkness, and broke away their chains."

REVEALED TRUTH

God is in love with those who are his. He created us and has always desired to walk with us in relationship. This truth is revealed in the creation of Adam and Eve. They were perfect in form, a genuine reflection of their creator. They were righteous and blameless, placed in the garden of Eden. Without affliction, adversity, and anguish, they were free to enjoy lives of unbroken fellowship with God. This is a picture that is far from reality today.

While Adam and Eve were in the garden, God revealed one thing to them. He told them not to eat of the tree of the knowledge of good and evil, for if they did, they would surely die. This warning was not a threat from God but was a statement of love. He knew their choice to eat from that tree would open their eyes to evil, breaking their relationship with him and unleashing the chaos of evil and death into their world.

The serpent in the garden used lying, manipulative words to deceive Eve into eating from the tree. He implied that Adam and Eve could be more than what they already were. The serpent implied that God was withholding good from them. Eve began to question their position and who they were. After much deliberation, Eve chose to eat the fruit, and then she gave some to Adam.

Immediately their eyes were opened to the knowledge of good and evil. They now saw things differently. Ashamed, they sought to cover themselves with fig leaves. Their decision to eat the fruit separated them from God and ended the pleasure of an unbroken relationship with him. This tragedy left all mankind separated and without God, struggling in their own efforts to survive.

Relentless in his love for mankind, however, God provided a covering for Adam and Eve through an animal sacrifice and the shedding of its blood. Today God offers us the gift of redemption and the covering of righteousness through a greater sacrifice—his Son, Jesus Christ. The shedding of his blood, when we accept him as Savior, removes our sin. This grants us the undeserved opportunity to be clothed in the righteousness of God in Christ Jesus. We can never earn this gift or work hard enough to accomplish it on our own. It can only be received through Jesus Christ. Salvation is a free gift from God himself. The only thing we must do is accept and receive it.

I know it can feel like we are the only ones struggling to survive in the grindstone of hardships and sufferings, but we are not alone. Hardships and hopelessness have been experienced throughout history. In the Bible, the children of Israel had lost hope, being bound by Pharaoh. Forced into slavery for hundreds of years, they cried out to God to save them. God heard their cries for help and set a plan of deliverance into motion to bring them out of their despair.

As I was bound, a slave to addiction, I felt like there was no hope of freedom. In my hopelessness, my heart cried out for help, and Jesus Christ responded and delivered me.

Are you faced with challenges today that lead you to believe there is no hope? God loves you and desires to save, rescue, and deliver you out of your trouble. Psalm 103:2–4 (ESV) says, "Bless the LORD, O my soul, and forget not all his benefits, who forgives all your iniquity, who heals all your diseases, who redeems your life from the pit, who crowns you with steadfast love and mercy."

A firm understanding of this truth will empower you to overcome the deception of hopelessness that says, "You are all alone!" "God doesn't care about you!" "You will never have a better life." This is far from the truth. We need to recognize and understand where these deceptive words come from and who is behind them.

Revelation 12:9 says, "The great dragon was hurled down—that ancient serpent called the devil, or Satan, who leads the whole world astray. He was hurled to the earth, and his angels with him."

It is the devil who whispers lying words like, "There is no God! If he were real, you wouldn't be suffering through all these hardships!" These lying whispers cause us to focus on our troubles, leaving us feeling hopeless!

I'm here to tell you, though, that God is real and he has a plan to deliver you and set you free! He has a plan that can transform your life. God is for you! He will hear your cry for help. He loves you. You can trust him.

When it appears as if God is not listening to your cries for help, be assured that he is. He alone is God. He knows all things. He sees all and hears all, especially your cry for help. When you call to him, be willing to surrender all to him, and he will break the chains that hold you captive. He will transform your life!

KEYS FOR YOUR FREEDOM

- Know that God loves you and desires to save, rescue, and deliver you out of your trouble!

  Bless the LORD, O my soul, and forget not all his benefits, who forgives all your iniquity, who heals all your diseases, who redeems your life from the pit, who crowns you with steadfast love and mercy. (Psalm 103:2–4 ESV)

- Believe that God will answer you when you cry to him for help.

  He shall call upon me, and I will answer him: I will be with him in trouble; I will deliver him, and honour him. (Psalm 91:15 KJV)

- Understand that Jesus knows your struggles, so you can approach him confidently, knowing that he will forgive you if you ask him.

  For we do not have a high priest who is unable to empathize with our weaknesses, but we have one who has been tempted in every way, just as we are—yet he did not sin. Let us then approach God's throne of grace with confidence, so that we may receive mercy and find grace to help us in our time of need. (Hebrews 4:15–16)

- Trust that God's love and intentions toward you are always good. You can trust him.

  "For I know the plans I have for you," declares the LORD, "plans to prosper you and not to harm you, plans to give you hope and a future." (Jeremiah 29:11)

Chapter 2
THE INTERNAL CONFLICT

Satan, who is the god of this world,
has blinded the minds of those
who don't believe.
They are unable to see the
glorious light of the Good News.
(2 Corinthians 4:4 NLT)

GOOD AND EVIL

I continued to ponder the question, "What are you going to do?" As I did so, a battle raged within me. I closed my eyes and thought about this man and his question. It made me wonder, *Who is he that he would care for me? If I don't know him, how could I have been calling him?* Yet somehow I could see his kindness and genuine care for me as he announced, "You have been calling me. Here I am!" I remember it felt so good with him there. Then I felt the painful contrast to this peaceful encounter with him as I felt the dark, ravenous, vicious grip and appetite of addiction. For the first time, I was face-to-face with the undeniable contrast of what was good and evil.

Although I had never considered the differences between good and evil before, I now felt the reality of their raging conflict. Yet even in that moment, I did not recognize good and evil being attributed to God and the devil. It was simply a fight between thoughts. *Can I give up drugs and hope for a life without them?* When I opened my eyes, I no longer saw the man who had been kneeling at my bedside.

As the internal war progressed, I kept thinking, *Can I give up this life I have always known? Is it possible to give up drugs—never to do them again? Will I be able to live a different life?*

I was so torn. I wanted to say yes to a life with this man, but I was afraid that I would find I wasn't strong enough to leave the life of addiction behind. I had already tried several times to stop using. I would give it up for a time and then foolishly believe that if I had made it a month without using, which seemed like such a conquest, surely I was in control. I would set out to pick up cocaine for that night, thinking, *I can do just a little bit and quit!* Surely I was in control now, right? Wrong!

As soon as I began to use, I would not stop until I had spent hundreds of dollars making up for the entire month I had gone without. These past failures were making it very difficult for me to choose to do the right thing when this man asked me what I was going to do. As I continued to go round and round with these thoughts, I began to drift back to sleep. Just as I was falling asleep, I heard his voice again saying, "Don't forget this."

The next morning, I woke up with my husband as he readied himself for work. I packed his lunch and made his breakfast without the slightest recollection of the events from the night before. After my husband left for the day, I did what was customary for me to do on days like that. I would turn the television to the music channel and crank up the volume as I began to clean up the mess we had made during the weekend.

In the process of cleaning, I gathered in a basket all the clothes that needed to be washed, and I headed down the hallway toward the washer and dryer. As I moved down the hallway, a voice came to me as if there were someone standing in front of me whom I could not see. "Don't forget last night!" the voice said. Without hesitation or fear, I responded, asking aloud, "Why? What happened last night?"

Instantly I saw what looked like a giant movie screen going up in front of me. It featured the events of the night before. I saw myself lying in bed crying and feeling the depth of pain inside, wondering why the tears were rolling. Now overwhelmed with emotion, I dropped to my knees and began to cry uncontrollably. Through the tears and labored attempts to catch my breath, I asked, "God—is this you? I mean—is—this—really you? Really God?"

I'm still unclear today as to why I would ask if it was God since throughout my entire life I had never even considered if he was real.

After a few minutes, the tears dwindled. I proceeded to pick up the clothes that I had dropped on the floor. I placed them in the washer and turned it on. I then busily pulled clothes out of the dryer to put in the basket. Heading down the hallway, I entered the living room, where the music was coming from the television. I turned the corner and everything around me disappeared. I was suddenly struck with tunnel vision as all my attention was focused on words that were pouring out from the television set: "My child has asked if her Father is there, and he is."

Without warning, my knees buckled underneath me and I dropped to the floor again. Clothes from the basket went flying everywhere as uncontrollable tears streamed down my face a second time. I was unmistakably made aware that these words coming from the television were a direct answer to the question that I had just asked in the hallway: "God, is this you?" How I knew this was the answer to the question, I'm unsure, but I was positive it was.

THE MOMENT OF CHOICE

Trying to reign in my emotions, I proceeded to pick up the clothes that I had dropped on the floor. I said to myself, *If I could just speak to my sister, I know everything will be okay.* At that very moment the phone rang, and at the same time someone knocked on my front door. I quickly dried my tears and answered the telephone with a quick statement: "Hold on; someone's at my front door." I set the phone down and headed for the front door. Opening it, I was rendered speechless. My sister was standing there.

I grabbed her by her coat collar and dragged her into my house with such force that I'm sure her feet were dangling in the air. I swiftly moved her into my living room and told her, "God has been talking to me all day!" With grief and desperation in her eyes, she looked at me as if to say, "What did you take?"

"I'm not high!" I was desperately trying to convince her that I was completely of sound mind. "God Almighty himself has been speaking to me!"

Again, I wondered why I would say "God Almighty," as I had never heard this term before. After sharing with her the events of my day, without any understanding of what I was doing or what was going to happen, I rose to my feet in the living room, raised both hands, and declared, "I'm done with drugs! I'm giving my life to God."

I had absolutely no idea what I was saying, as I did not know if God was real. I did not know him, and I had no idea what it meant to give myself to him. I was thrilled that at that moment I could answer his question without hesitation. I meant every word I had just spoken. At that moment, God broke the chains, and I saw the tyrannical addiction for what it was—slavery.

Now that I had been set free, you would think I would have taken every precaution to stay far away from that lifestyle. Regrettably, with bad choices it didn't take long before I found myself face-to-face with temptation only a week after my deliverance. A friend asked if I wanted to go to the bar to shoot darts. Seeing nothing wrong with going to have fun, I went. Not long after arriving, a mutual friend walked in. We both knew him well, for he had supplied drugs for us many times.

He walked over and began to play darts with us. After about an hour, my friend approached me and said, "Yvonne, he wants us to go over to his house to play games there. Do you want to go?" I was hesitant, realizing that drugs would be present. With that in mind, I should have turned to run. Instead, I said, "Sure." I was determined that I would say no if they offered me drugs. What was I thinking?

Thirty minutes after our arrival, my friend walked toward me with a mirror in her right hand loaded with lines of cocaine. In her left hand she held the straw. With an amused grin on her face, she leaned over and said, "Here. Want some?"

I instantly replied, "No!" To my amazement, there was no desire present within me, and my refusal was not one of "white knuckles."

For the next several minutes I was bombarded with clamoring statements like, "Come on!" "It's just one line!" "Who cares?" Then I was taken by surprise as I saw the look in my friend's eyes change into an ominous glare. Her tone changed as she said, "Just take it. No one will know! We won't tell!" Contempt filled her eyes as she pressed for my participation. "Fine! Just take half of it then!"

My anger grew with every pressing push until I said, "Get out of my face! I told you I don't want it! If you want to take this outside, then let's go; otherwise, back off! I don't want it!"

With her final look of disgust, the fight was over. She reached over and took the cocaine for herself. I know that was the moment God sealed my deliverance. Although that battle was over, I had no idea that something else was just ahead.

THE TRADE

Over the next few days, my drinking exponentially increased. I would drink from the time I got up to the time I went to bed. After weeks of this consistent behavior, my husband voiced his concerns. He, too, had been free from drugs, having made the choice not to do them again. He was not a big drinker. For weeks he silently watched as I carelessly jumped into a life filled with alcohol. Day after day I spent all my time drinking with friends. One morning as my husband prepared for work and I, of course, was getting ready to go to my friend's house yet again, he sat down to put his boots on. He looked at me with compassion and hurt in his eyes as he said, "How do you think this makes me feel, watching you trade one drug for another?"

Mysteriously, as I heard my husband's voice, I simultaneously heard the voice of the man who had stood by my bedside. I heard him asking me through my husband's words, "How do you think this makes me feel?" I don't know how this was possible, but I heard him clearly nonetheless.

When I heard this, I took a good hard look at the things I had been doing. Upon examining the recent weeks of my life, I could see nothing but destruction. I was completely self-absorbed, leaving my family unattended as I soaked myself with liquor. At that moment, my heart was devastated as I realized the damage and the hurt my choices had caused over this short period of time. My life had been a drunken blur for which I had been completely responsible. At that moment, I knew that I would have to be honest with myself, with my husband, and with this man I had encountered. I had indeed traded one drug for another, and it had quickly formed chains in an attempt to hold me captive.

As I looked at my husband, my heart ached as I observed the pain my actions had caused. Looking into my husband's eyes, again I miraculously and mysteriously saw the eyes of the man who stood at my bedside. I was acutely aware of the deep sorrow I had caused both of them, and I was overwhelmed with grief.

In hearing the question, "How do you think this makes me feel?," I knew I was facing another moment that had the potential to impact my life with a change for good. I just needed to make the right choice. As I examined myself—my actions and attitudes—with a sincere heart, I simultaneously responded to both my husband and the man with a single reply: "I'm sorry. I won't drink again." Immediately those chains were broken, and I put away the alcohol. I had no idea my decision would lead to yet another challenge.

THE DECEPTIVE VOICE

The following day, I headed out to the grocery store. I needed to pick up a few things for the evening's dinner. As I walked into the store, I grabbed a grocery cart and headed for the food aisle. As I proceeded toward the food, immediately to my left were three aisles of liquor. As I stepped in front of these aisles, I heard an audible voice speak to me. I turned to look, only to see an aisle with no one standing in it. Then I heard the voice again as it shouted, "Come on!"

This voice was nothing like the gentle, caring voice I had heard before. This one carried a demeaning tone. It was malicious, and I could hear the implication of pleasure it had in its taunting as it continued, "Come on, get one bottle! You know you want me! Come on! Just drink me!"

I asked myself, *What is happening? How could these bottles of alcohol audibly speak to me? Am I truly losing my mind?* As I continued to walk past the aisles, I addressed the voice that seemed to be coming straight from the liquor bottles. With an infuriated tone, I said out loud, "No! I don't want you!"

I marched away from the aisles of alcohol mumbling under my breath and filled with anger. While shopping, I thought about those statements: "You know you want me. Just drink me!" The hard reality hit me that I was not angry because these statements were trying to tempt me, but I was angry because they were right. I did want that bottle! I wanted to pick it up and take it home. I wanted to drink it. However, more than wanting to drink that bottle, I wanted to keep my word to my husband and to the man I saw.

As I left the store, my eyes were opened to see the demonic influence behind the alcohol. Fighting against its allure that day, I became excruciatingly aware that liquor had taken the reins of addiction and I would have to fight for my freedom.

For the next several months, every time I stepped into a grocery store I would hear the deceptive voice of alcohol calling to me. It was relentless in its campaign of enticement, and I remained persistent in my refusal to participate. With a consistent refusal to give in and a constant effort to remain faithful to the words I had spoken to my husband, the alcohol began to lose its power—until one day it no longer had a voice. Now I understand the spiritual reality behind alcohol being called spirits.

Why did God deliver me from drugs but then leave me to fight for freedom from alcohol? I now understand. God has the power to supernaturally deliver us and set us free. However, he also wants us to know that he has given us power to fight against temptation and break the chains of captivity.

REVEALED TRUTH

It is God's desire to share in our lives, both in good times and in times of trouble. This truth is revealed in the account of the children of Israel in the Bible. God's heart was to release them from their captivity and bring them into a trusting relationship with him. From their limited perspective, it would appear that God had forgotten them. In their forced labor, it would be easy to draw the conclusion that God was not listening. Yet that was far from the truth. God was busy orchestrating their deliverance as he prepared a deliverer.

Jesus Christ is our deliverer. He paid the price of his own life to rescue us from the power of Satan. We no longer have to remain in a hopeless existence. We can experience his supernatural power to break the chains of bondage and transform our lives.

KEYS FOR YOUR FREEDOM

- Believe that God and the devil are more than a concept. They are real, and God has destroyed the works of the devil, who fights for the possession of our souls. God has sent Jesus to be our deliverer.

  The reason the Son of God appeared was to destroy the devil's work. (1 John 3:8)

- Understand that the choices you make today will determine the outcome of your life and freedom.

  Today I have given you the choice between life and death, between blessings and curses. Now I call on heaven and earth to witness the choice you make. Oh, that you would choose life, so that you and your descendants might live! (Deuteronomy 30:19 NLT)

- Know that trials will come, but also know that you can remain in peace as you trust in what Jesus has done for you.

  I have told you these things, so that in me you may have peace. In this world you will have trouble. But take heart! I have overcome the world. (John 16:33)

- Trust that every time you submit to God and resist temptation, your deliverance is sealed.

Submit yourselves, then, to God. Resist the devil, and he will flee from you. (James 4:7)

Chapter 3
SPIRIT REALM REVEALED

Be alert and of sober mind. Your enemy the
devil prowls around like a roaring lion
looking for someone to devour.
(1 Peter 5:8)

DEMONS: IMAGINATION OR REALITY?

After Jesus appeared to me the second time, I began to see things in the spirit realm. At the time, I had no idea that there was a spirit realm and that demons were real. I didn't know how to make sense of everything I was witnessing. Anyone who may have their thinking strictly rooted in the natural realm (as I did), only understanding the world through logic and reason, would say that the experiences I'm about to share with you had "insanity" written all over them. That is why I would often ask myself during this time, *Am I losing my mind?*

Today I completely understand that my sanity and my perception of this natural world were never in question. I was simply gaining insight into the reality of the spiritual realm and the evil that exists within it. This evil can gain access into our lives through the things we participate in as we live our lives without Christ.

The witchcraft, drugs, and sexual immorality that I had participated in gave an open invitation for the forces of darkness to wreak havoc and hold me captive. The things I saw were like gross creatures out of some horror movie. In my ignorance of their existence, the forces of darkness were able to work against me and influence my thoughts and actions, completely undetected by me. Without understanding all that I was experiencing, I knew this for sure: these creatures were no longer hidden, and their working against me turned into something completely heinous, leaving me petrified.

It began with glimpses out of the corner of my eye. I would see sudden movements, like something running across the floor or shooting across the ceiling. Not understanding what I now know as seeing in the spirit realm, I simply used my human understanding to reason it away. However, the glimpses didn't stop. I thought, for example, that it just must have been a spider—only to look and find nothing there. This continued for several days, growing into something bigger.

One evening after putting our daughters to bed, my husband and I decided to grab a blanket and lie down on the sofa to watch a movie. After getting the pillows and blankets, we turned off the lights and started the show. When the movie was over, we turned off the television and just started talking in the dark. It wasn't long before we made ourselves so comfortable that we decided to sleep there for the night.

While lying there talking, I noticed a black streak shoot across the ceiling. I thought it must have been a shadow from the headlights of a car that was passing by. I kept seeing the dark streaks flash across the ceiling, though, and realized these shadows were not created by any light source from the street. I looked back up to the ceiling and saw several shadowy figures swishing through the air in all directions across the ceiling. Again, I can't explain how I knew this was an evil supernatural experience, but I was completely aware that I was afraid of it.

For a split second while lying there with my husband, I thought about asking him if he could see what I was seeing. I quickly decided that I had better not. I thought that if I told him what I saw, he would question my sanity. Then I thought, *If I tell him, he'll just give me a logical explanation for what I am witnessing.* I mean, even I tried to explain it away.

Was it all my imagination? Was there really a logical explanation for these things? I often found myself in a panic, wondering what was happening. I could not explain the sudden voices that alcohol, drugs, and even nicotine had obtained. I did not understand how they were speaking to me. I had no idea why I was able to mysteriously see these dark shadows flying in my home. Many times I would ask myself the question, *Is my husband seeing all these strange occurrences but, like me, just not saying anything about them?* I quickly shut those questions down and determined to walk through this alone.

Over the next few days, I began having a series of terrifying dreams. These dreams were so incredibly vivid that they will be forever burned into my memory. In my first dream, I was in my bedroom sitting on the end of my bed that was next to the window. I stood up to walk across the room and noticed a dark silhouette of a man standing in the shadows of the carport just outside my window. I couldn't make out a face or the details of his stature. In my struggle to identify this person, I became fearful that he would see me. I was acutely aware that I needed to keep myself hidden.

Horrified, I suddenly realized this person now knew I was standing in the window behind the blinds. While he was glaring at me through the glass, I could feel evil coming directly from him, and it pierced right through me. I stood frozen as the presence of this darkness penetrated the room where I was standing.

I knew this person was now after me and that his intentions were very evil. Filled with absolute fear, I slowly began to back away from the window, hoping this person would just forget about me. As I took a step backward, it seemed as if someone were suddenly in the room with me. Too terrified to look, my instinct was to turn and run to get out of the room. In pure desperation, I promptly turned toward the door and began to run.

Just as I reached for the doorknob, I felt the evil presence directly behind me. I quickly turned around. As I did, I noticed a creature in the upper left corner of the room. It had large dragon-like wings that stretched from one wall to the other. Its talons were incredibly long and sharp, like daggers. The creature's horns extended upward from the top of its head, and his face was riddled with deep crevasses as he scowled. His gruesome stare penetrated right through me. Without hesitation, he lunged toward me. In utter panic, I raised my arms to cover my head. Instantly, a sword appeared in my left hand and a shield in my right. This hideous creature bounced off the shield.

Then suddenly I woke up, filled with absolute terror as my heart felt like it was pounding out of my chest. With several deep breaths, I labored to calm myself. Once my emotions were quieted, I got up to start the day.

For days, I could not shake the feeling of being chased. Nor could I forget the grotesque creature that lunged for me. It became difficult for me to fall asleep at night, as I did not want to go through another terrible nightmare—but I had a second dream a few days later. In the dream, I was standing inside a house that I didn't recognize. The house was dirty and was filled with dust and cobwebs. Intertwined with the cobwebs were spider webs that covered every square inch of this dwelling place.

As I looked across the room, I saw a white high-top Converse tennis shoe. It caught my attention because it was sitting on a display ledge that was carved into the wall. As I walked over to the shoe, I tried hard not to touch the webs. Wondering why the shoe was so out of place, I wanted to get a closer look. Who would choose to display a tennis shoe?

As I reached out to grab the shoe off the wall, I was startled when a white translucent spider jumped up out of the top of the shoe. It seemed as though this spider was guarding its territory. It jumped out at me, not wanting me to touch the shoe in any way.

As I turned to walk away from this spider, I now realized that there were spiders everywhere, all their eyes focused on me. Each time I would try to move, they would try to block me in. Immediately I thought, *I don't want to be here!*

As quickly as I thought this, I woke up in yet another fright. I was desperate for all this to stop, but instead, I fell asleep and had yet another nightmare. In the third dream, I was standing in a room that appeared to be on the top floor of a house. It looked as if someone had remodeled an attic and turned it into a bedroom. As I stood in this room, a gigantic spider came out of nowhere. Its enormous body was the size of a small melon, while its legs were incredibly small—completely disproportionate to its size. Despite its peculiar size and shape, the spider was incredibly fast. It started running.

At first I tried to dodge it, thinking it was running after me. Then I realized it was trying to get away from me and hide. I made the decision that I was not going to be afraid. I pursued it, determined to kill it. This entire dream consisted of this pursuit. Somehow this gigantic spider evaded me at every turn until it ran under a jewelry box and got away.

I woke up wondering what all this meant, and I would continue to wonder this for a while. The next evening produced the most perplexing dream of all. In this dream, I was standing in the center of a white movie screen. An enormous python was wrapped around me, squeezing me as hard as it could, trying to keep my arms pinned to my side. I struggled back and forth with the snake, thinking, *If I could just get my arms out, I would be able to get free from the grip of this vicious thing.*

Unaware of how I got loose from the python's grasp, I was suddenly standing there holding its mouth in my hands. I was pulling with all my strength until its jaws were dislocated and torn apart.

Once again, I woke up with my heart pounding rapidly and my breathing labored. At this point, I was exhausted from the constant onslaught of attacks within my dreams. Night after night, I found myself in tears, feeling the persistent crush of hopelessness that had wrapped itself around me. These nightmares truly struck terror in my heart. I was left with an overwhelming sense that they would never cease.

My dreams had never been like this before. I had hardly ever had nightmares, and they certainly had never been terrorizing in nature. I began to wonder what had changed so drastically that I would be plagued with dreams so full of horror that I would wake up in a panic. Now I realize that all this began the moment I made the choice to give up drugs.

Hosea 4:6 says, "My people are destroyed from lack of knowledge." It took me a long time to understand that God sometimes speaks in dreams and visions. His purpose is always to help us gain understanding, especially when personal changes, direction, and instructions are needed. In my dreams, God exposed the cost and result of sin that had been buried deep inside me. With each dream, he would reveal my spiritual condition and bring me to a place where I understood that I was completely and utterly lost without Jesus Christ.

I don't think I ever would have considered light and dark, good and evil, or God and the devil—until the demons began to manifest right in front of me. I was forced to confront the reality of evil face-to-face.

STIR UP THE GIFT

Wanting a reprieve from terrorized nights, I began staying up late to watch the Trinity Broadcasting Network. I continued watching their programs night after night. I remember one late night hearing a man named Kenneth Copeland talk about stirring up the gift within you. He concluded his talk by saying, "I have a message on tape that will help teach you to walk with God and grow spiritually in your relationship with him." All I had to do was call the number and request a copy. Without hesitation I called, having no idea what it meant to live for God, let alone how to grow spiritually.

Shortly after I made the call, I received the cassette in the mail. Printed on top of the cassette was simply, "Stir up the gift." I found my cassette player, took out the tape, and began listening. Kenneth Copeland began by saying, "Stir up the gift." An onslaught of questions filled my mind. *What gift? How do I stir it up?* Though understanding eluded me, I continued listening, hoping that something would eventually connect and give me insight. My cassette player had an auto-reverse option so that the tape would play continuously. As I was listening in bed, I eventually fell asleep, while the cassette continued to play throughout the night.

The next morning, I woke up filled with absolute fear and trembling. Somehow the words of the message touched something dark that was deep down inside me and left me shaking to my core. The anxiety was ruthless and dominated the day. I found myself pacing the hallway like a caged wild cat wanting to get on the other side of the bars that held it captive. I kept trying to calm myself down, but no matter how hard I tried, I could not find the peace I was desperately searching for and needed at that moment.

I realize now that it was a demonic hold.

The evening before this event, I had made arrangements to drive to Seattle to take my mom out for a nice lunch. However, after waking up plagued with this inner torment of terror, I had no idea how I would get into my car to drive. The very core of my being was shaking violently, as if an earthquake was occurring inside me. This sudden encounter with fear and anxiety left me in no condition to drive. I had never experienced such panic before. I was hit with one rushing wave of adrenaline after another, rendering me powerless to catch my breath. *Please, somebody, help me!*

Although this was the cry of my heart, I never said it out loud. I knew an audible cry for help would leave me with no other option than to reveal all the things that were happening to me. I feared that no one would understand. They would simply think I had lost my mind. I didn't even think my husband would believe me, so I made the decision to go through this without saying anything to anyone. Although this was another spiritual experience, it was not like the days prior; it was much more violent internally.

I remember thinking, *Before my husband begins to ask questions, I need to calm myself down.* I thought that if anyone were to find out about this, they would surely put me in a straitjacket, lock me up, and throw away the key. I couldn't explain the things I was now seeing and the voices I was now hearing.

With extreme levels of anxiety that unremittingly persisted, I began to feel as though I would be physically sick. I went to my room and sat down at the foot of my bed facing the corner. As I looked up into the corner of the ceiling, I did the only thing I could think of: I called out, "God."

Instantly I was taken somewhere, whether in a dream, a vision, or a trance, I don't know. One thing I knew for sure—I was no longer in my room. I was in what looked like a cavern. However, as I observed my surroundings, I realized there was neither an entrance nor an exit. It was like I was being held inside some enormous boulder.

Fire stood directly in front of me. I looked to my right and saw a witch's cauldron. There were ladies standing around it, and I could hear the muttering of incantations coming from their direction. Then, in the center of this place, there was a grotesque display of all sorts of sexually immoral acts being carried out. To the left was a party scene with people who were being ravaged by drugs and alcohol. Deceived by its enticing lure, they couldn't see the demons that had now taken them captive. Oblivious to the evil behind all of it, they were now slaves to this horrific demonic-filled lifestyle and the trauma that went along with it.

I stood in this place scrutinizing every detail of each scenario as I observed it. After viewing all this, I knew these were scenes of the sins of my life. The witchcraft, sexual immorality, addiction, and the lifestyle of lying, cheating, and stealing were all the things that had been recorded against me.

Suddenly I saw what looked like a massive paddle, shaped like a boat oar with a very short handle, suspended in midair above the fire. Then, as if it were being held by an unseen hand, the flat end of the oar was lowered and placed into the flames. Watching intently as the oar sat in the fire for some time, I studied it as it was finally lifted up out of the fire. It seemed as though the oar was completely unscathed by the flames, but then it turned toward me, revealing the opposite side of the oar. Etched into the wood by the flames was one single word: "ABRAHAM." *Who is Abraham?* I thought. *What does it mean?*

As I continued to watch, suddenly a hideous face appeared before me. Laughing with great amusement, he was relentless in his taunting. He took great pleasure informing me, without words, that this was where I would spend eternity. His mocking, condescending nature revealed the enormous pleasure he found in the fact that he had been able to deceive me throughout my life. At that moment, he was boastful in his assurance that he had been incredibly successful in his plan to deceive and destroy me. Haughty in his demeanor, he was confident that this would be my final destination.

I had bought his lies! The occult activity—the tarot cards, Ouija boards, bloody Mary, attempts of levitation—they were nothing more than innocent childhood games. Sexual sin was a harmless indulgence. Drugs were just a means to have a good time. I was convinced that I wasn't hurting anyone. These were all simple pleasures just for fun. Certainly there was nothing spiritual about what I was doing. I found out that this was exactly what the devil wanted me to believe.

There is a divine reason why the Lord tells us to keep from these things, and it's not simply to keep us from having fun, as many would think. He knows the hideous evil and hidden destruction that we are exposed to if we indulge ourselves. If we take part in these activities, whether deliberately, ignorantly, or blindly, they will eventually demand a price for our participation.

God's desire is beyond just saving, healing, and delivering us. He desires that we would become his children and live under his covering of righteousness. In the first part of John 10:10, Jesus said, "The thief comes only to steal and kill and destroy." That was exactly what Satan was doing to me—with one tormenting situation after another, until I thought I was losing my mind! I had nowhere to run and no place to hide from the agonizing onslaught of terror. Overwhelmed by the terror, I failed to recognize that Jesus had come to give me something greater than my current existence. In the remaining portion of John 10:10, Jesus revealed, "I have come that they may have life, and have it to the full."

It is God's great love for us that desires to keep us from evil destruction and within the borders of his protection. We are fooled into thinking, though, that God just wants to keep us from enjoying the pleasures of life. That is very far from the truth. It's the same insinuating lie that the serpent told in the garden: "You don't need to obey God. He is holding out on you because he knows if you eat of the tree of the knowledge of good and evil, you will be like him, and then you won't need him." The devil's purposes and schemes never change, but the way they are presented might change.

Without knowledge of this spiritual truth, I had been deceived! I believed that my participation in drugs, cultic games, and sexual sin was just mere pleasure. Now I would come face-to-face with the reality of the price that would be demanded.

I stood paralyzed with fear as the devil's gruesome face continued to laugh at me, mocking and taunting me with every gesture. I was overcome by a tremendous sense of grief and sorrow. All I wanted was to get out of this place, but as I said before, there was no exit. I didn't even know where I was, let alone how to get out. Struck by horror and fear, I tried to call out the name of Jesus. I don't know why that was the name I turned to, considering that I knew nothing of him. Nonetheless, all I could get out was "Jes . . ." It felt as if someone's hands were around my throat squeezing my vocal cords and trying to keep me from speaking his name.

With every turn of my head trying to break free from the grip around my neck, I could only manage to say, "Jes . . ." Determined not to give up, I kept fighting to speak—until finally out of my mouth I managed a loud shout: "Jesus!" I kept saying his name over and over again. I'm not sure how many times I called his name, but suddenly, *whoosh*, I was back in my room, sitting at the foot of the bed where I had initially sat down.

I immediately began to cry as I screamed out, "What is happening to me?" Then in an instant, I felt two arms wrap around me from behind, cradling and rocking me from side to side. I could feel the gentle patting of a hand on the side of my left upper arm as I heard a gentle whisper into my left ear, "*Shhh.* Everything is going to be okay now!" Then it felt like a bucket of warm oil was being poured over my head and flowing all the way down to my feet.

As inexplicably as the fear and terror had arrived that morning to haunt me, it was just as inexplicably gone with the pouring of the oil. I was overwhelmed by a gentle comfort that permeated every part of my being at that moment. I was not too quick to move from this place, as I quickly realized it was a sanctuary of utter peace and a desperately needed reprieve from the torment.

After several minutes, I turned and looked at the clock and thought, *I have plenty of time to drive to Seattle, pick up my mom, and treat her to a very special lunch.* I was elated as I thought about the words that had been spoken to me: "Everything is going to be okay now." I interpreted that to mean I was not going crazy—and all these tormenting occurrences were over!

The spiritual realm is not just a fictitious idea created in the imaginations of those who would populate Hollywood's screens with their tales of hell, devils, and demons. It is a reality.

As I prepared to head out for lunch with my mother, it would only be a few minutes before I would understand the lengths that God went to in order to deliver me and set me free.

REVEALED TRUTH

Being inundated with demonic images throughout cultural history has desensitized us to the reality of the spiritual realm and its demons. Hollywood has covered the theatrical screens with images of the devil, demons, and hell to the point that these things are not taken seriously.

They leave us with the idea that the spiritual realm is fantasy, just a form of entertainment.

After Jesus Christ appeared to me a second time, I was submerged in the reality of the spiritual realm. Beyond my natural understanding, I was seeing into this spiritual realm that exists—with God and his angels and Satan and a force of demonic spirits. Its reality is presented in the Word of God and reveals how this demonic force works.

John 10:10 reveals the intent of this enemy: "The thief comes only to steal and kill and destroy." As with any battle, it's important to understand how the enemy works against us. It is through lying suggestions that the enemy seeks to manipulate our thinking, twisting and confusing the thought process to manipulate our behavior.

The goal is to bring forth destructive behaviors that lead to ruin, leaving us destitute, broken, and without God. If the devil can keep us unaware of his influence and manipulations, he can keep us from the knowledge of God and his truth. He works diligently against humans because even he knows the power of God and the power of his Word!

The Bible declares that the Word of God is alive and powerful, sharper than a two-edged sword (Hebrews 4:12). There is nothing more powerful in our lives than when we are walking with God and are being obedient to his Word. When the Word of God is in our hands, it becomes a spiritual sword. This sword is a weapon that is full of power and causes demons to shudder. As long as the devil can get people to question the reality of God and his intentions toward mankind, we will remain impeded and open to Satan's schemes of destruction.

When God created mankind, he gave them the garden of Eden and every tree to partake of, except one—the tree of the knowledge of good and evil. The serpent labored constantly to cast shadows on the integrity, character, and intentions of God.

The results of his efforts left Eve believing that partaking of this one particular tree, which God commanded Adam and Eve not to eat, was not really bad at all. The serpent implied that eating the fruit was actually a good thing. It would make Eve wise and like God. So, under the serpent's influence, Eve considered the sly serpent's suggestions. Satan targeted her desires through the lust of the flesh and the desire to be wise. She yielded to the serpent's lies, ate of the fruit of the tree, and also gave it to Adam to eat. This series of disobedient actions left Adam and Eve subject to the penalty of death, and they instantly died spiritually, no longer covered with the glory of God.

The deception of this demonic force is not limited to lying words, for as we see in the Bible, demons also try to manipulate human behavior. Great examples of this truth can be found throughout the Bible. In 1 Samuel 18, King Saul was tormented by an evil spirit and tried to kill David. In Mark 5 we read about the man who lived in the tombs, who couldn't even be held down by chains. In Mark 9 there's a man whose son was possessed by an evil spirit that caused him to get rigid and foam at the mouth and who was thrown into the fire by these demons.

If we don't fall prey to the devil's deception the first time, he'll try to find another way. He may use suggestions like "There is no God" or "No one can judge you." If he can't get you to fall for that, he will try to make you believe that the entire spiritual world is fictitious, saying things like "It's not real," "It's just your imagination," "You're going crazy," or "What will people think if you tell them what's happening to you? They will lock you up and throw away the key!"

The spiritual realm is a reality. Within it is an army of demonic forces that have been defeated by Christ Jesus. Although their defeat is sure, they do not stop at their attempts to deceive God's people as they lead them astray with lying suggestions such as "Go ahead and do it; it won't hurt you," "Nobody will know," or "It's not wrong!" The only goal of these demonic forces is to kill God's people, steal their hope, and destroy their lives. However, Jesus Christ came and destroyed the works of the devil. Jesus took from him the keys of hell, death, and the grave. Then Jesus Christ received all authority, and he gave it to those who would believe in his name, trust that he died to redeem them, and receive him as Savior.

With lying words, these demonic forces can catch people unwittingly off guard, and the result is the devastating absence of God's presence in their lives. This demonic reality is after one thing: the destruction of people and their lives. But Jesus Christ said, "I have come that they may have life, and that they may have it more abundantly" (John 10:10 NKJV).

KEYS FOR YOUR FREEDOM

- Realize the spiritual realm is real and there is an enemy who seeks to destroy.

  Be alert and of sober mind. Your enemy the devil prowls around like a roaring lion looking for someone to devour. (1 Peter 5:8)

- Know and trust that Jesus Christ is God. He came to earth to break the power of the devil and set us free from Satan's power.

  Since the children have flesh and blood, he too shared in their humanity so that by his death he might break the power of him who holds the power of death—that is, the devil. (Hebrews 2:14)

- Run to God, and he will help you stand against the devil's temptations.

  Because he himself suffered when he was tempted, he is able to help those who are being tempted. (Hebrews 2:18)

- Understand that occult games open spiritual doors for demonic forces! Don't give the devil access to your life.

  Do not give the devil a foothold. (Ephesians 4:27)

- Know that we have been given authority over all the power of the enemy. Take it!

  I have given you authority to trample on snakes and scorpions and to overcome all the power of the enemy; nothing will harm you. (Luke 10:19)

Chapter 4
THE GOSPEL

*For God made Christ, who never sinned, to
be the offering for our sin, so that we could
be made right with God through Christ.
(2 Corinthians 5:21 NLT)*

NO ORDINARY DRIVE

As I kept track of the time, I got ready to head out for my mom's house. That morning had been a rough one for me. Mascara running down my face, tear tracks in my foundation, and puffy bright-red eyes placed a clarion call that freshening up was definitely in order. After washing my face and reapplying my makeup, I made a solid effort to try to hide the evidence of all the crying I had just done. I put my jacket on, grabbed my keys, kissed my husband, and shouted "I love you!" as I closed the door behind me and ran to the car.

I was ready to get away and take a much-needed break from these chaotic days that had consumed my entire week. I wanted to escape from the torrential rains of terror and was looking forward to spending quiet quality time with my mom enjoying a good lunch and girl talk. As I headed down the street, I decided to forgo the freeway and just take the route through the city. It was approximately twenty miles to

Mom's house from mine, so I figured it would take me about thirty minutes to get there.

Still six miles from my destination, I approached a street light in Seattle as the light turned red. As I was at a full stop waiting for the light to turn green, all of a sudden there appeared before me what looked like a giant movie screen going up. It covered the windshield of the car, and I was caught up into yet another vision. I observed the earth suspended in space and being cut vertically in half from top to bottom. Then the front half of the globe was removed and set next to the other half. I could see the center of the earth and all the different layers—from the topsoil to the bedrock to the core.

Then the image of the earth focused in on one half as it hung in front of me. As I looked at the earth, the image zoomed in and I could see something very small, but I couldn't clearly identify it. The picture zoomed in again, and I could see a cross standing by itself on top of the earth. With another zoom, I could see a man hanging on the cross. He had been nailed to it.

Unexpectedly, I saw this man come off the cross just like he was floating. He began descending through the different levels of the earth. When he reached its depth, he stretched out his right hand and took hold of three gold keys. Then he turned to face me and locked his eyes with mine. As he stood there with the keys hanging from his fingers, I was instantly filled with the knowledge that Jesus had come to die and gain possession of these keys. He had done it all for me.

I watched as this man began to ascend back through the different levels of earth. However, since he had possession of the keys, he didn't return to the cross from which he had descended. Instead, he bypassed the cross and continued to ascend to heaven. He stood there before God and presented his blood from the cross and these three gold keys. While watching these events take place, each frame was being explained in great detail without words; it was supernatural.

For the first time, by revelation from God himself, I understood that Jesus was the man on the cross. As the Son of God, he relinquished his divine power as God. He willingly came to earth in the form of sinful flesh. Although he lived a sinless life, he was willing to die like a criminal through death by crucifixion so that he might redeem his creation and restore to us the covering of righteousness that was lost in the garden of Eden.

As I watched the vision before me, I was painfully aware that it was my life of sin that had put Jesus on that cross to die. It was my life of sin that drove those nails through his hands and feet. Though it was my sin, Jesus paid the severity of punishment for my sin with his life. Romans 6:23 says, "For the wages of sin is death, but the gift of God is eternal life in Christ Jesus our Lord." Without working for it or trying to earn it, I was freely given eternal life by Jesus through his sacrifice on the cross, covering me in the righteousness of God.

With great love for mankind, Jesus endured separation from his Father to die a sinner's death and descend into the depths of hell. In Jesus's descent, his mission to regain possession of the keys of the power of death, hell, and the grave was successful. These keys became Satan's when mankind chose rebellion—Satan's way of living—over obedience to God. By completing this mission, Jesus redeemed mankind and reconciled us to a loving relationship with God as his children. Hebrews 2:14 (KJV) says, "Forasmuch then as the children are partakers of flesh and blood, he also himself likewise took part of the same; that through death he might destroy him that had the power of death, that is, the devil." For the first time in my entire life I was given the gospel with complete understanding. I believed it!

Instantly I was back in my car, tears streaming uncontrollably down my face yet again. I was overwhelmed with an amazing sense of security. I understood the magnitude of his unconditional love for me and for all of mankind. Absolute joy filled my heart as I thought, *Jesus loves me! He died for me! My sinful life nailed his body to the cross, yet he loves me anyway! How could this be?*

As I wiped away the tears, I realized I was two blocks away from my mom's house. I had absolutely no recollection of driving. I was still approximately six miles up the road when I stopped for that red light. How did I get here? I had no idea! I just decided there were so many supernatural things going on that I was not going to trouble myself trying to figure it out. I was okay and the car was okay, so I collected myself, wiped my face, and headed into Mom's house. For the rest of the day, I held on tight to the vision that had been shared with me.

After lunch, I spent a few more hours visiting with my mom before I headed home. After I arrived home, I prepared dinner for my family. I concluded the day with our daily routine and made sure that everyone was safely tucked in bed. While enjoying the peace and quiet in the house at the end of the day, I was absolutely in awe of the things I had been shown and was looking forward to life.

CRUCIFIED

The first thing on my mind the next morning when I woke up was a book I had just received, titled, *Behold I Give unto You Power* by Paul E. Billheimer. As I opened the pages, I began to read the accounts of Jesus's life and sacrifice he had made to redeem mankind from destruction. It confirmed everything I had been shown in the vision. Excited, I walked into the kitchen to get my morning cup of coffee. I quickly moved to the living room to make myself comfortable on the sofa. Opening the book, I immediately began to read about being crucified with Christ.

Well, this made no sense; I had never been hung on a cross. Then, in great detail, the writer explained Galatians 2:20, and I began to understand: "I have been crucified with Christ and I no longer live, but Christ lives in me. The life I now live in the body, I live by faith in the

Son of God, who loved me and gave himself for me." Elated, I thought this was yesterday's vision in writing!

As I continued to read about Christ being crucified, the writer began to talk about overcoming the devil. Although all these strange things were happening to me, I had only recently learned that there was a devil. Needless to say, some of these new concepts began to make me feel uncomfortable. I was now certain that I wanted nothing to do with the devil. He had already made sure that I knew he would be there to torment me forever.

Then I read, "And they overcame him by the blood of the Lamb and by the word of their testimony" (Revelation 12:11 NKJV). As I was reading this verse, out of the corner of my eye I saw something scoot across the floor just in front of me. I looked up from my book to see this massive beige demon lying on the floor. It had a face that looked like a man's, yet it was incredibly deformed and monstrous. It had short arms with enormous claws extending from its long, lanky fingers. This creature had no legs. It simply looked like its body had been torn in two, leaving the lower part of its extremities shredded like ribbons that hung from its waist.

Without legs, the demon would move across the floor by reaching forward with its claws, sinking them into the carpet and pulling itself forward. As I looked at it the very first time, it did not speak verbally, yet somehow I could hear what it was thinking.

It never took its eyes off me, and I realized it was waiting to see if I would react to it in any way. As I continued to look, I could hear it thinking, *Did she see me?* I just stared at it with no reaction. It thought again, *No, she didn't see me!* At that point the creature reached out again, sank its claws into the carpet, and pulled itself closer to me, again thinking, *Did she see me?*

With that second movement, the creature was entirely too close to me. Petrified, I brought my feet up onto the sofa as quickly as I could.

Shutting my eyes, I began to rock back and forth, thinking, *I don't want to be here. Please, not again!* Without a word, I could hear the unspoken communication of this cynical creature as it thought, *Come down off the cross! Come down here.*

Without a single rational thought, I just screamed back at it, shouting, "No, I will not come down! I was crucified with Christ, and I will not come down!" I can only imagine what my neighbors must have thought at this point. They knew I was home alone, yet I was yelling loudly enough for all of them to hear.

I continued to scream, "I will not come down!" I then realized that I was no longer in my living room. I found myself standing in utter blackness. It was so black that I could not see myself standing there. *Where am I?* I thought. I kept trying to look around, but I couldn't see anything. Then I began to hear a distant thundering. I became aware of the rumbling of the blackness around me as it began to shake. The blackness was being pulled down from the center of its existence by a hand that could not be seen. As it was being pulled straight down, the rumbling became greater, until the blackness was released like a slingshot. As it shot up into the air, the blackness was annihilated with a tremendous explosion. This explosion caused the blackness to utterly disintegrate into fine dust particles. With the annihilation of the blackness, a red color rolled down the side of this place from top to bottom. Quickly following the red, white began to wash over the entire place.

As I watched this scene unfold—the blackness shooting upward exploding into dust and the red and white washing over it until all that was left was a space covered in pure white—I immediately understood what I was being shown. I knew that the blackness was all the sin and evil that had dominated my life. It had now been annihilated by the blood of Jesus, which was the red. The power of the Holy Spirit was the explosion, which lasted until there was nothing left but righteousness. This was the white.

After being shaken from this trance or vision, I was suddenly back in my living room, aware of my surroundings again. I could hear myself repeating over and over, "And they overcame him by the blood of the Lamb and by the word of their testimony." Once again in tears, I found myself questioning my sanity. While sitting there crying, I stammered, "God, I'm scared! I don't know what's happening to me." With that, I suddenly saw a man sitting on the other side of my L-shaped sectional sofa. I was sitting on the long side, while this man was sitting on the shorter side, to my right.

He appeared to be like the man who had been at my bedside those two times. However, this time when he turned and looked at me, there was an evil glare in his eyes that scared me to my core. *You are not Jesus!* I thought, and with that, he disappeared right before my eyes.

I began thinking, *I can't take anymore of this! I'm ready to turn myself in!* Feeling hopeless and emotionally out of control, I stretched out on my stomach and buried my face in the sofa. Without lifting my face, I began to see everything around me as though I had my head lifted and was looking around. While I lay face down on the sofa, I saw another man standing right there next to me. This time I could see him to my left from the waist down. He was wearing the same white robe that I had seen before. It was radiant, as if the sunshine was coming straight out of it. Without moving, I could also see down to the floor, and I saw his feet and the sandals he was wearing. His feet looked like bronze in color, yet somehow I could see straight through them. On each foot, up toward the ankle, was a hole where he had been pierced through. I also saw the lower part of a royal-blue sash that draped over the bottom side of his beautiful white robe.

As I continued to observe this man who was standing beside me, he became a pillar of smoke. With a single gentle movement, this pillar of smoke rose up from the floor and ascended into the air. It then came down over the sofa and entered into the center of my back. As the pillar of smoke went through my back, I literally felt it flutter on my stomach as it was pressed against the sofa.

I sat up. As I did, I did not hear a voice, but I heard the thoughts of that beige demon with no legs as it said, *That was me! You better tell me to leave you! Tell me to get out!* For a split second I listened and was just about to say it, but then I had another thought: *No, that was God!* Out of my mouth I exclaimed, "No, that was God! I will not tell God to leave me!"

Thankfully, soon after these events things began to change for the better. I no longer felt as though I was walking through a living nightmare. Over the next month, I was filled with an uncontrolled desire to pick up the Bible and read. As I read each word, situations around me began to make much more sense.

STEPPING INTO CHRIST

Now that I had given my life to Christ and had a fuller understanding of who he was and the price he had paid for my redemption, I looked forward to living life for him by jumping in with both feet. We never really understand our life experiences until we have walked through them. Only in retrospect do we clearly see the reasons.

From the time I was eight until this moment when I surrendered my heart and life to Christ Jesus at the age of thirty, my life was filled with darkness. Through the rituals and traditions of my Native American culture that was intertwined with deceptions, my family went down many different avenues to find power and some sense of peace in life. Unfortunately, our journey led us into diverse lifestyles like witchcraft, transcendental meditation, and addictions. Eventually, through the love and grace of my heavenly Father, I was introduced to what it means to seek God. My participation in the worldly pursuits and traditions never really brought me closer to the Lord, but they in fact kept me from the deep intimacy that I so desired to have with him.

Not fully understanding, I began to ask him questions: "God, if my heart desires to be close to you and to live for you, how do I get there?" I honestly believe that this is a secret cry of many hearts before the Lord. Questions like this become a focus as the Lord brings us out of the lives we once lived, moving us from the kingdom of darkness into his kingdom of light.

To love God and live a life grounded and rooted in him begins with the knowledge and understanding of who he is. To be victorious in life, we must also have a firm understanding of who we are in him. It was not long after I began asking questions like this that the Lord revealed another spiritual truth to me. This revelation would yet again transform my thinking and the way I lived. God gave me another dream, sharing a truth that would aid tremendously in steering the course of my life, even to this day.

The dream began with a blank black screen, silent and still. Then brilliant glistening stars began to appear until millions of them hung in space. I found myself surrounded by them, as though I were standing in the middle of space itself. As I was standing in awe, gazing at the splendor of my surroundings, I saw the Lord ahead of me in the distance.

Once I caught a glimpse of him, I stood still. He opened his arms to me as if to say, "Come to me." I began walking toward him, no longer mesmerized by the surrounding environment. My full attention was on him as I continued to walk. I did not slow my pace nor avert my attention from him. As I approached him, instead of stopping in front of him, I stepped into his being.

My perspective changed, and I was now watching myself from a distance as I stepped into Christ. I could see that I was in Christ and Christ was in me. Instantly, I woke up understanding the dream. My thoughts went to the place where Jesus prayed for those who would come to believe in him based on the testimony of those who had gone before them. He prayed "that they all may be one; just as You, Father, are in Me and I in You, that they also may be one in Us" (John 17:21 AMP).

How amazing! The grace of God can instantly take me out of my life of sin and place me in Christ Jesus and his righteousness.

It is difficult for us to comprehend the depth of this truth with all the different challenges we face in life. I am no exception. Although God had given me a dream and I understood the facts of what he was telling me, I did not have revelation—a deeper spiritual understanding—of the impact of this truth on our lives.

It astonishes me how, in our own efforts, we complicate the simplicity of the spiritual truths of salvation, healing, deliverance, and transformation. We believe we must work to be righteous, but 2 Corinthians 5:21 clearly informs us that "God made him who had no sin to be sin for us, so that in him we might become the righteousness of God."

It is vital that we take the Bible at face value. We must understand that what God said is what he meant. Complicating it through our earthly perspective can keep us from receiving revelation of his truth. When we come to the Word with childlike faith, we will know our righteousness in Christ Jesus and will view ourselves from his perspective as the creator of the universe. Accepting the simplicity of his truth will bring about our deliverance.

REVEALED TRUTH

When I consider all I have learned, it leaves me asking some questions:

- How do we manage to obtain the wrong picture of God and question his character toward us after we are saved?

- Why do we become so unsure of his love for us?

- When we do something wrong, why do we expect God to be angry and upset with us? Instead, we should rest in his truth: "But God demonstrates his own love for us in this: While we were still sinners, Christ died for us" (Romans 5:8).

We have been given the privilege of coming boldly into his presence without fear! On that astonishing day when he said, "Come to me," my life was filled with addiction. I was a sinner in the midst of a cesspool of sin. Yet in my room, as I stood in his presence, Jesus Christ held no judgment against me. He looked at me with eyes of love and compassion.

How much more should we trust him who has saved us from the wages of sin? The truth that he is God, the one who loves us, should be enough to keep us secure as we stand and live in his presence each day.

KEYS FOR YOUR FREEDOM

- Know that it was Jesus's love for you that kept him on the cross to die a sinner's death, although he himself was without sin. Be reconciled to him.

  We are therefore Christ's ambassadors, as though God were making his appeal through us. We implore you on Christ's behalf: Be reconciled to God. God made him who had no sin to be sin for us, so that in him we might become the righteousness of God. (2 Corinthians 5:20–21)

- Believe with your heart that Jesus died for your sin and was raised again to life. Then confess Jesus as your Lord, and you will be saved.

  If you declare with your mouth, "Jesus is Lord," and believe in your heart that God raised him from the dead, you will be saved. For it is with your heart that you believe and are justified, and it is with your mouth that you profess your faith and are saved. (Romans 10:9–10)

- Trust that God has a plan for you—even when you can't see it.

  "For I know the plans I have for you," declares the LORD, *"plans to prosper you and not to harm you, plans to give you hope and a future." (Jeremiah 29:11)*

Chapter 5
HOLY SPIRIT INTRODUCTIONS

All of them were filled with the Holy Spirit and
began to speak in other tongues
as the Spirit enabled them.
(Acts 2:4)

MY FIRST EXPERIENCE

Acts 19:2 tells us that Paul encountered some disciples and asked them, "'Did you receive the Holy Spirit when you believed?' They answered, 'No, we have not even heard that there is a Holy Spirit.'" This was my experience as well. Although a disciple of Jesus Christ, I was completely unaware that there was a Holy Spirit or that he was to have an active role in my life. John 16:13 says, "But when he, the Spirit of truth, comes, he will guide you into all the truth. He will not speak on his own; he will speak only what he hears, and he will tell you what is yet to come."

I had no knowledge that the Holy Spirit is the Spirit of Christ. I had no understanding that he was the transforming power that would change me from the inside out. Although I was oblivious to the Holy Spirit's reality, he began to initiate brief encounters with me. I was quickly aware of his presence, but still had no idea who he was.

Eventually, through the following series of experiences, I would come to know the person of the Holy Spirit and his desire to help me grow in my relationship with Jesus.

My introductions began by feeling the weight of his presence come upon me. It was foreign and frightening, as it caused me to feel numb. Of course, being led by my natural feelings and reasoning, the floodgates of fear were thrown wide open. This initiated bombarding thoughts like, *Why are my arms numb? Wait—isn't this what heart attack victims feel? What if . . . ?* Of course, this line of thinking sustained an increase of adrenaline that exponentially magnified the fear. Panic and shortness of breath now required that I spend the next thirty minutes talking to myself, trying to calm down.

Looking back at these experiences, I find myself laughing, because I was afraid due to a lack of knowledge. With each individual experience, I would search the Bible to understand. Through the process, I learned how much I needed the Holy Spirit in my life. When I accepted Jesus's sacrifice on the cross for me and declared Jesus Lord of my life, the Holy Spirit came to take up residence within me.

The Holy Spirit is always there to guide me through the trials and issues of life. When I'm hurting, I can talk with him and he brings me comfort. When I'm unsure of situations, he guides me in the way I'm to go. Through my relationship with the Holy Spirit, my life has taken on a new dynamic that I wouldn't trade for anything. He has become a trusted friend—one who helps, empowers, and transforms my life.

HIS GUIDING PRESENCE

One night while I was on my way to church, I was driving with two of my daughters and my brother. Waiting at a red light, I happened to look in my rearview mirror and saw a car quickly approaching us. When I realized it was not slowing down, I found that I was unable to speak to warn my family of the impending impact. I locked my arms as I held on to the steering wheel, pushing myself into the back of the seat to brace for impact.

With my adrenaline pumping, there was a thunderous clash of banging metal as the car behind us drove straight into my car without the driver hitting his brakes. My first thought as I was listening to the crumbling of metal was, "My car!" Using my imagination, I envisioned the whole back side of my car demolished since we had been hit hard enough to be pushed over the crosswalk and out into the intersection.

Suddenly, with a surge of panic, I checked on my family. Then I jumped out of my car and rushed to the driver of the car who hit us. As I approached the car, a man got out with his hand on his forehead. He wiped his forehead in disbelief as he slurred out the words, "Oh man, are you okay?" It became obvious that the man was completely intoxicated, as he stumbled around just trying to stand still. Slurring his words, he tried to apologize. I asked him to pull his car over to the curb while we called the police to ensure that everyone was okay.

As I was heading back to my car, I felt that same weight come upon me as before. The thought occurred to me that we needed to get the license plate number of the other car. I yelled out to my brother to write it down. As he was writing, I pulled my car off the road. I kept looking into the rearview mirror to keep my eye on the other driver, only to watch him take off and head for the freeway. Fortunately for us, we were only two blocks from the police department, so we went there and filed a report, giving a full description of the man who was driving, along with the color, model, make, and license plate number of the car.

The next morning, I woke up to a tremendous amount of pain from the base of my skull to the middle of my back. It wasn't long before I was informed by the doctors that the trapezius muscles in my back had been torn and severely damaged by the impact because I had braced so hard against the back of the seat instead of allowing myself to roll with the hit.

For the next several months, I was forced into bed rest so the muscles could heal. During this time, I spent hours on end reading the Bible. It was then that my encounters with the Holy Spirit increased, although I was not aware of what was truly happening. I sometimes wonder if the Lord found humor in my responses as I was introduced to the Holy Spirit.

HIS TANGIBLE PRESENCE

One morning during my period of bed rest, after my husband departed for work and my children were on their way to school, I put myself back into bed since the pain that morning was unbearable. With tears filling my eyes, I was constantly adjusting myself, trying to find a way to hold the Bible and read without bringing about so much pain. I stacked as many pillows as I could at the head of the bed, trying to alleviate the strain on my shoulders and neck as I leaned back into them.

With my arms propped up with pillows, I leaned back on the ones behind me and held the Bible straight out in front of me. My arms would get tired, but I could hold them up much longer with the aid of the pillows than I could by sitting straight up and looking down into the book. As I was reading, I had my first encounter with the tangible presence of the Holy Spirit.

Have you ever been asleep and then woke up because you sensed someone standing in the room watching you? My encounter with the Holy Spirit was much like this. As I was reading and holding the Bible up in front of my face, I suddenly felt someone in the room with me. I knew that I was the only one at home, so instantly I panicked.

Like a scene one might see in a scary movie, I slowly began to lower my arms as I raised my eyebrows to see over the top of the book. I was certain that I would find someone standing there. As I peered over the book, I was relieved to find that I was alone. Without any further thought, I went back to reading.

Again it felt as if someone had walked into the room. My heart began to race once again as I slowly moved the book to see over the top, only to find no one there. I thought, *That is so weird.* Lifting the Bible up one more time, I continued to read, only to sense that presence again. This time it was more than just feeling the presence, I could actually feel heat on the back of my hands as I held the Bible. It was as if someone were so close that I could feel that person's body heat.

Terrified, I was temporarily paralyzed in fear! The thought of moving was horrifying to me, as I was sure there would be some unsightly face just on the other side of the Bible. Gradually, I lowered my Bible with my eyes bugged out in anticipation of who or what was on the other side. To my surprise, there was no one there. I laid my Bible down for a moment to shake off the fear. I tried to slow my heart rate down, which was completely out of control. At this juncture, I told myself, *It was just your imagination. Settle down!*

As I lifted up the Bible again, I was quickly captivated by the words printed on the pages, with no further thought of these incidents. Suddenly, there it was again—the undeniable presence of someone in that room with me. The returning intense heat on the back of my hands communicated to my brain, *Whoever it is, they are very close.*

This time I looked as I set my Bible down, but I couldn't see anything or anyone—yet the presence remained in the room. I was so petrified that I began to back up on my bed to try to get away from this presence. With nowhere left to go, I literally crawled up onto the bookshelf headboard of our bed. I'm sure my eyes were as big as saucers as I asked, "Who are you?" Not really wanting an answer, I just closed my eyes and instantly sensed that this presence was gone.

It was just after this encounter that I was watching Christian television. A preacher began to speak about the presence of the Holy

Spirit. This pastor shared about how wonderful the Holy Spirit is and spoke about the reality of his presence. I began to think of a thousand questions: *Is there really a Holy Spirit? If so, what is it? What does this preacher mean when he speaks of the Holy Spirit's presence?*

The next program on television was a movie about the birth of Jesus. I was completely mesmerized by the accounts of Mary's experiences with the Holy Spirit as they were depicted on television. I know they were theatrical liberties, yet I was captivated by the actress who played the role of Mary and her portrayal of such a genuine reaction to the presence of the angel of the Lord as he delivered God's message.

That dramatization helped me draw the conclusion that everything I was experiencing was in fact the presence of the Holy Spirit. Mary's reactions in that dramatization were so exact to my own encounter that I began to ask the question, *God, was that the Holy Spirit who was in my room?* This movie caused me to think more about the Holy Spirit and to study what the Bible had to say about him.

MARCHING FOR JESUS

The "March for Jesus" event in Seattle was coming up in a few days. I had made arrangements with my brother, sister, and a few friends to go on this walk. I was excited about participating, as this was a way I could declare my faith in Christ. That morning, a group of us drove into Seattle to the starting point of the walk. We got everything we needed from the car and met with thousands in the park. We spent the day walking, talking, and singing. I felt like I was on top of the world. No longer bound by addiction and no longer seeing strange creatures in my home, I was growing in faith. I was free—and I was free to proclaim it!

As we finished the twenty-mile walk, people were heading toward their cars. My brother, his girlfriend, and her children were getting ready to leave. They asked if my daughter could ride home with them.

"Sure! I will meet you there," I answered. Still in the company of my sister and her boyfriend, we headed to the parking lot together. As we walked through the park toward my car, we were approached by three women. One of them grabbed me by the arm and asked, "Have you received the Holy Spirit since you believed?" I was shocked. *Who is this strange woman, and why is she grabbing me?* Though I heard her question, I was unsure how to answer. I simply shrugged my shoulders. My sister and her boyfriend then walked away.

Another woman asked me, "Have you been baptized with the Holy Spirit?" I had no idea what they were talking about. I would later learn that they were referring to Acts 1:5, when Jesus said, "For John baptized with water, but in a few days you will be baptized with the Holy Spirit." A third woman quickly interjected, "Do you speak with other tongues?" The second woman added, "Do you want to?"

Feeling a bit overwhelmed by the ambush of questions, I stood there speechless. Again the women asked, "Do you speak with other tongues?"

"No," I answered.

"Would you like to?"

I thought, *Well, what am I supposed to say now? No?* With a bit of hesitation, I said, "Yes."

Before praying with me, these three women explained in detail how Jesus sent the Holy Spirit to be a helper to us. They elaborated how the Holy Spirit would teach us the things we needed to know. John 14:26 says it like this: "But the Advocate, the Holy Spirit, whom the Father will send in my name, will teach you all things and will remind you of everything I have said to you."

The three women continued to share with me how Jesus baptizes us and gives us a gift of speaking in tongues, a new language that we could use when speaking directly to God. I had no clue that everything they were saying to me was straight out of the Bible. Later during my times of study, I found that Acts 2:4 says, "All of them were filled with the Holy Spirit and began to speak in other tongues as the Spirit enabled them."

These excited women asked me to bow my head. Though I was uncomfortable, I bowed my head to pray with them to ask for the baptism of the Holy Spirit. While I was standing there, they began to speak what sounded like gibberish to me. I opened one eye to watch them, thinking, *Okay—this is weird!* I stood there not knowing what to do, so I remained silent. After about fifteen minutes, they stopped speaking these funny utterances and said, "Well, you just keep asking. You'll get it." And off they went.

What in the world was all that? was the only thing I kept thinking as I walked back to my car. My sister and her boyfriend were waiting as I approached my car.

"Thanks a lot, guys, for sticking around with me!"

They began to laugh as they recalled the look on my face as I was ambushed by those women. On the drive back home, I began to think about the movie I had seen, the presence that I had experienced in my bedroom, the teachings of the preacher on television, and now the aggressive but fervent actions of these women in the park. Could it be there was something to all this? Could there be something to the experience the women referred to as the baptism of the Holy Spirit?

I arrived home, got out of the car, went into the house, and hurriedly greeted my family. I could not stop thinking about the Holy Spirit and all my recent encounters related to this subject. I couldn't wait to find that quiet private space where I could be alone and speak to the Lord about it. After greeting everyone, I went straight to my room, fell down on my knees, and began to pray.

God, I don't know if what those women spoke of in the park is true. I don't even know if it is in your Word. However, if it is and it really is from you, then I want it! If what they told me is truly a gift from you, then I'm asking you to baptize me with your Holy Spirit and give me the gift of this new language, the new tongues they told me about.

This may seem incredibly careless to some, but in a childlike manner I asked God for everything these women had shared with me before I ever read it in the Bible for myself. Something inside of me hoped for it.

For days I prayed, asking God many questions: *Is the Holy Spirit real? Does he really have a genuine desire to be part of my life? Is this ability to speak in a new language really a gift from him? If he is real, can I know him the way I have come to know Jesus?*

My prayers persisted for the next several days. I prayed about the baptism of the Holy Spirit every morning, every afternoon, and every night before bed. Wanting to know about the Holy Spirit was all I could think of or ask during that period of searching.

While being persistent in asking God my same questions, it seemed as though everyone on television began speaking about the Holy Spirit. They would say things like, "He is a friend to us" and "We can talk with him just like we talk to Jesus." This only fueled my desire to know him for myself.

After nine days of bombarding God with the same questions, I still had no concrete answers regarding the reality of the Holy Spirit. By this I mean that I had not yet experienced anything these women had shared. Sure, I was suddenly hearing everyone on Christian television speak about the Holy Spirit, and some Christian movies I saw focused on the topic of the Holy Spirit. Though all this was happening, none of it would prove the Holy Spirit's reality to me. If it were true, I wanted my own experience with him.

I know now that every event, every television show, every movie, and even the women in the park were all strategically and supernaturally orchestrated. God was ushering me into an ordained moment with the reality of the Holy Spirit.

On the tenth day of my pursuit of the reality of the Holy Spirit, I was filled with desperation. I had spent every day recalling the things I had heard about the Holy Spirit. Every hour of pondering echoed the same question: "Is it true?" The time I spent asking and seeking for his truth created an unquenchable longing in my heart. *God, please! If it is all true, grant it to me!*

Overwhelmed by the aching of my heart, I knelt down on the floor and rested my head on my bed. With tears streaming down my face, I prayed, *God, if all I have heard about the Holy Spirit is true, please show me. If he is real and it is possible to sit and talk with him the way I do with Jesus, then I'm asking that he come and talk with me.*

With my face buried in the mattress of the bed, I became aware of a presence that entered the room through the exterior wall. The thought instantly went through my mind to open my eyes and look. My next thought, though, wrapped in fear, said, "No way!"

There was a full-fledged argument going on inside me. *Turn and talk with him!* I thought, only to have my answer continue to be the same: "No!" Finally, this warm presence left the room the same way it came in. As it left, I opened my eyes and turned my head to look, only to find that it was gone. I was kneeling there alone.

My next thought was, *Yvonne! You have been asking God about the Holy Spirit. You asked God to have the Holy Spirit come and talk with you if he is real! Now you didn't even bother to open your eyes or acknowledge the fact that you could sense his presence in the room while he was here! Now it's too late, and you will never know if it was him!* Though I was completely upset with myself, I was not going to allow this to keep me from my pursuit.

THE BAPTISM

On day fourteen of my pursuit, I began with a continued bombarding prayer to God for the baptism of the Holy Spirit. The day went by quietly as my children were in school and my husband was at work. I spent the day cleaning, doing laundry, and preparing for the evening's meal. It was a normal day.

When my children arrived home from school, we sat down to do homework. As soon as they were finished, they watched television until it was time to wash up for dinner. Shortly after my husband came home at five, we all sat down together at the table for dinner. Every evening, the conversations began with my husband asking the children, "So how was school?" This is a question that we continue to ask our grandchildren today.

After dinner, we entered into our evening routines for the next few hours. After everyone bathed, got in their pajamas, and brushed their teeth, we tucked the children in bed for the night. With my husband in our bedroom fast asleep, I seized the moment to spend quiet time with God. It was my routine to go into our spare room to be alone with the Lord. Sitting down on that bed, I propped myself up with a pillow as I reclined back on the headboard, stretching out my legs to read for a while. This was my opportunity to again ask God for the baptism of the Holy Spirit and the gift of tongues. Only this time, it became evident that something was happening as I asked.

I felt that weight come upon me again like it did when the accident occurred. This time it was much more intense. I remember thinking, *What's happening? God, I'm scared!* I instinctively tried to lean forward to lift my back from the bookshelf headboard. I felt as though I was unable to move anymore under this heavy weight.

God, I'm scared! I can't seem to move! Why?

With much struggle, I bent my legs and folded them together. I then tried to lift my back off the headboard so I could sit straight up. The moment I was able to lift my body away from the headboard, my body continued in a forward motion. Still unable to lift my hands or move my arms, I continued in a forward motion until I fell face first into the mattress. I had felt this numb feeling before, but not quite like this. I was struggling to move. Now face down, I was thinking, *God, what is this?* As I had this thought, I tried to say it out loud. When I opened my mouth, strange words came out of me. It actually startled me when I heard what I uttered. *Did I just say that?*

As I opened my mouth to speak to the Lord, a language foreign to me poured out. I thought, *This is it! This is what those women told me about! God, this incredible gift of baptism with the Holy Spirit and the gift of a new tongue truly is from you!*

First Corinthians 14:2 says, "For anyone who speaks in a tongue does not speak to people but to God." With this new language, I wanted nothing more than to stay right where I was and speak to God. I continued speaking for hours, when suddenly the Holy Spirit began to show me internal pictures of my childhood. He began to reveal times and places throughout my childhood where he was actively working to bring me into a loving relationship with Jesus. He showed me the elderly woman, Clara, who used to live next door to me when I was eleven years old.

The Holy Spirit reminded me of all the times Clara said things to me like, "Look at how God painted the sky today." He showed me in every one of her statements that he was working to gain my attention. He told me about the tiny Bibles Clara would give my little sister and how he was there pursuing me every time my sister showed me what she had received.

Then I got one of the greatest surprises I could have ever hoped for: the Holy Spirit showed me how he was the one who had moved Clara's heart to pray for me and my family. He led her to pray that God would work in our lives and make a way for us to come to know his love. He granted me glimpses into the hours, the days, and the years that she faithfully prayed for me. Overwhelmed with gratitude for the loving care of God my Father, the sacrifice of my Savior Jesus Christ, and now the power of the Holy Spirit working for me, I sat with a stream of tears running down my cheeks, mixed with joy as I pondered his work.

I'm so blessed to know that God was actively pursuing me long before I came to know him. I'm duly honored to know that a woman who really didn't know me, other than watching me and my friends play in the street or giving me a quick wave "Hello!" as I ran by her house, would present me to God every day as she prayed. Now I fully enjoy the transforming goodness of God through the power of his Holy Spirit. This was something Clara knew and enjoyed herself and desperately wanted me to know.

After receiving all the insight regarding Clara, I again began to speak in my new language. As I was speaking, I began thinking, *I wonder what I'm saying.* Then supernaturally I began to hear the foreign words I was speaking, in English. I was filled with emotion as I heard the words, "Holy, holy, holy is the Lord God Almighty who was and is and is to come. Holy, holy, holy is the Lord God Almighty who was and is and is to come." Miraculously, I knew that though I was speaking in a language unknown to me, these were the words that were being declared!

The Bible speaks of this incredible miracle in Acts 2:7–8: "Utterly amazed, they asked: 'Aren't all these who are speaking Galileans? Then how is it that each of us hears them in our native language?'" Astonished by the proclamation, I crumbled into a gut-wrenching sob as I realized that he who is and is to come has loved me, saved me, and has now filled me with his Spirit. What can I say but "Holy, holy, holy is he"? He has blessed me with a gift of great magnitude, a gift that could never have a price assigned to it, and a gift that cost him his life to give to me. From that time on, whether washing dishes, taking out the trash, scrubbing toilets, or just sitting, I was always praying and speaking with him in this new language.

I spent hours speaking in tongues every day after that. I began to experience spiritual growth in leaps and bounds. Then one day as I was spending time with God praying and speaking in tongues, I heard this strange voice say, "Oh! You've just cursed God. Now you are going to be cursed for what you have said. If you only knew, you would never speak in this language again! Now you will be condemned for what you have uttered."

Fear and panic gripped me as I heard these words! *God, I'm so sorry if I have said anything against you.* If I had said something to curse my God, I would give up this new language. Then, with a broken heart, I purposed never to pray in tongues again. I did not want to speak against God ever.

After about three days had passed, I began to experience a very disturbing feeling within, as if something significant was suddenly missing. I could not identify what it was, and I wasted no time in going to God. I asked, *Lord, why do I feel this way?*

I was prompted to examine the past three days and take note of anything I was doing differently. I reviewed the three days many times and always came to the same conclusion. The only thing different was that I had stopped praying in tongues. However, when I thought about speaking, I became fearful.

I was compelled to pick up my Bible. As I did, it opened to Romans 8:26–27: "In the same way, the Spirit helps us in our weakness. We do not know what we ought to pray for, but the Spirit himself intercedes for us through wordless groans. And he who searches our hearts knows the mind of the Spirit, because the Spirit intercedes for God's people in accordance with the will of God." There it is! These words shined like a neon light: "In accordance with the will of God"!

When I read these words, I began to study them inside my heart: "In accordance with the will of God." Now I know it is not God's will that I would ever curse him, and if the Holy Spirit gives me the utterance, I know he would never speak forth a curse. If that is true, then I could be confident he was helping me put into words that which my heart could not communicate in English. While drawing these conclusions, the Holy Spirit opened my eyes to see the lie of the devil. I quickly spoke out loud, "I see you, devil, and your lies! You stopped me for the last three days, but you won't stop me again!" Immediately I began praying in tongues, and I instantly felt whole again, as the missing piece had been put back in place.

This is why it is so crucial that we are planted and rooted in the Word of God. Satan tried to twist the Word of God and use it against Jesus during his forty days in the wilderness when Jesus was being tempted by Satan. Jesus, being full of the written Word of God, successfully deflected each temptation and each demonic twisting of God's Word. If being rooted and grounded in God's Word was necessary for Jesus here on earth, how much more necessary is it for us? With this understanding, I perceived the importance of the Word of God in my life and of the ability to recognize and follow the Holy Spirit.

STUDY CONGRUENCY

Shortly after learning this important lesson, I was ready to move forward in my prayer time. One morning while preparing for the day, I thought, *I have a ton of things that I must get done today. I'm not sure if I can achieve it all in the short amount of time I have.* Then, without missing a beat, my thoughts were quickly interrupted by a very deliberate and purposeful thought: *Yvonne, stop and pray; spend time with God, and he will make your path straight.*

After hearing this, I stopped what I was doing, went into my library, and took a seat in the chair. I grabbed my Bible, my journal, and a pen as I quieted my mind. Then I said, *God, my day is packed full of things I need to get done. However, I want to start it with you. What would you have me do today?* Clearly and without delay, the Holy Spirit said, "Study congruency!" I knew for sure that this was the Lord, as I had never before used the word *congruency*.

With that, I got up from my chair, walked to the bookshelf, and reached for the dictionary. I looked up the definition of *congruency* in order to understand what God wanted me to do that day. As I began to study this word, I was directed to other words that collectively began to paint a beautiful picture that would reveal the depth, as well as the importance, of congruency in my spiritual life with the Holy Spirit.

Then, in a vision, I saw a river that was softly flowing as the waters gently made their way downstream. With this picture, the Holy Spirit revealed that he was the gentle water and that he wanted me to come into agreement with him. I made a deliberate choice and entered into this agreement. He leads and I follow, knowing that he leads me in the ways of righteousness. I thank God for this amazing promise of the Holy Spirit.

REVEALED TRUTH

In the beginning, God formed Adam and placed him in the garden of Eden to tend it. Adam had an amazing unbroken fellowship with God. Adam was given authority to reign over God's creation, with the instruction that he was not to eat from the tree of the knowledge of good and evil. It was now in Adam and Eve's hands to trust God's love for them and choose to follow him above their own understanding, knowing he had the best planned for them.

As long as Adam and Eve chose to remain in God's love and obey his instructions, the authority was theirs to demonstrate. In their freedom to choose, Adam and Eve partook of the tree of the knowledge of good and evil and surrendered their authority to Satan, releasing sin and death into the world.

Since then, mankind has been subjected to the evil plots of the devil, who only seeks to steal, kill, and destroy the very thing that God loves—mankind. However, Jesus Christ came to destroy the evil works of the devil and to liberate us from the demonic chains of captivity by dying a sinner's death so that we might be redeemed from the tyrannical control and destruction of the devil.

Upon his death, Jesus paid in full the penalty of death for all who would put their faith, hope, and trust in him. In his burial, descending into the depths of the earth, he took the keys of death, hell, and the grave. When Jesus ascended to heaven, he presented his blood and the finished work of his cross to his Father. It was then that God sent his promise of the Holy Spirit for those who would be his.

It is impossible to change ourselves. We can try and make an attempt in the strength of our flesh, but we would not achieve the kind of change we desperately desire. Trying and failing only produces a discouragement that leaves us frustrated and blinded to the possibilities of who we could be.

God never meant for us to walk through life trying to change ourselves. This is the very reason he made a way to provide a helper for us. It is our responsibility to cultivate a relationship with the Holy Spirit in which we learn to follow him. It is only in following him that the power of the Holy Spirit can bring true, lasting, supernatural change to our lives. Second Corinthians 3:17 says, "Now the Lord is the Spirit, and where the Spirit of the Lord is, there is freedom."

I remember the day that the Spirit of God led me to study this Bible verse to find the depth of its meaning. A conversation ensued as the Spirit of God began to ask me questions in order to lead me to the truth. It began when he asked me, "Where is the Spirit of the Lord?" I thought, *The Spirit of God is everywhere!* Then very quickly another question arose within me: *Then why are so many people still in bondage?*

That question made me realize that the Lord must have been saying something much more significant than what I was reading on the surface. I immediately began to search out what was being indicated in this statement. I began to search out the Greek word for each word in this verse.

Without giving a lengthy explanation of every step I took, let me get to the truth that was revealed. As I studied the word *is*, I was made aware that this word does not just mean "existence." In fact, *is* comes from the Greek word that means "to be, or to become."

When I thought about this, the Holy Spirit asked me, "To be or become what?" I was a bit puzzled by this question since I was not exactly sure what he was asking. I began to dig deeper into God's Word. My search led me to Exodus 3:14, where God told Moses, "I AM who I AM." The word for *'I AM'* is the same Greek word for *'IS'* meaning "to be or to become." Then, by revelation of the Spirit, I understood that when I permit the Spirit of the Lord to be Lord in the moment of my trial, I allow him to lead while I follow, and that is where I obtain true freedom.

Lasting transformation and freedom will escape us if we try to accomplish these things in our own strength. The Bible declares in Zechariah 4:6: "'Not by might nor by power, but by my Spirit,' says the LORD Almighty." If God went to the extent that he did to provide the help of the Holy Spirit, wouldn't it be to our advantage to follow him?

KEYS FOR YOUR FREEDOM

- Know that when you obey the Holy Spirit in moments of temptation, you make him Lord of your life—and that is where you will find your freedom.

  Now the Lord is the Spirit, and where the Spirit of the Lord is, there is freedom. (2 Corinthians 3:17)

- Understand that the Holy Spirit is here to help you and teach you the truth. Remain in him and in his Word.

But as his anointing teaches you about all things and as that anointing is real, not counterfeit—just as it has taught you, remain in him. (1 John 2:27)

- Recognize that your transformation will only be to the degree that you yield yourself to his leading.

  For if you live according to the flesh, you will die; but if by the Spirit you put to death the misdeeds of the body, you will live. For those who are led by the Spirit of God are the children of God. The Spirit you received does not make you slaves, so that you live in fear again; rather, the Spirit you received brought about your adoption to sonship. And by him we cry, "Abba, Father." (Romans 8:13–15)

Chapter 6
HEARING HIS VOICE

Today, if you hear his voice, do not harden
your hearts as you did in the rebellion.
(Hebrews 3:15)

IT TAKES FAITH

Through casual conversations, I have heard many people say that they do not hear the voice of God. It saddens me to think that anyone would miss out on hearing God speak. Confessing that you cannot hear the voice of God can create detrimental feelings of not measuring up. It can become a perpetual weight when people feel they are missing out on the supernatural experiences others are having.

The question may be asked of me, How could I possibly know the pain of not hearing his voice if I had been hearing his voice before I was saved? Although this may be a reasonable question, I think it is the very reason that made my learning and combat for faith so difficult. Each whispered demonic lie clouded my understanding and blinded me to the reality that I knew and heard his voice. Believing I could not hear God's voice left me distracted in an already arduous quest to understand what I was experiencing and why.

When I began to hear God's voice, I was completely oblivious to the fact that it was him speaking. Unfortunately, being unaware allowed doubt and unbelief to gain ground in my life as I struggled in my process of learning to trust God. One challenge after another afforded me the opportunity to engage my faith. Missing the mark of faith time and again gave birth to moments that were pure agony. I continued to be bombarded by an onslaught of doubt in my pursuit to hear his voice.

During the course of being educated by God through the Holy Spirit, I learned to ask God to speak to me. I now know that I must be willing to engage my faith and trust that he is, in fact, speaking. Through this learning and growing period, I had to learn how to hear him.

NOT WITH PHYSICAL EARS

Through the progression of experiences, I have come to understand the power that doubt and unbelief can have in blocking our way. These two characteristics are the major hindrances we face as we set out to establish our relationship with God. This fact was made evident as I read in the Word of God that we are not to have an evil heart of unbelief. At first, learning this truth only added to my feeling of defeat. The devil would twist the Word of God in an attempt to cause me to believe that I was already a disappointment to God. The fact that I didn't trust God only sealed my fate as I saw myself as evil and inept. The devil is our enemy. His demonic goal is to tell us lies that leave us feeling like no matter how hard we try, we will never be good enough to walk in close fellowship with God. Once we believe that deception, it is impossible to hear God's voice when he speaks.

It was only by the grace of God that my eyes were opened to recognize that the devil, that evil serpent, has used this tactic from the beginning of time. He works to make us feel insecure in our relationship with God. The goal of this deception is to see ourselves as inferior when we examine who we are in our relationship with the Lord. However, the great news is that our relationship with God is not about what we do to succeed in it, but our relationship with God has everything to do with Jesus Christ. What he has done clothes and covers us in his righteousness so that our unrighteousness is never seen by God.

It was with this truth that I realized I was covered by Jesus and cloaked in his righteousness. Through his sacrifice for me on the cross, I am not evil, but am made the righteousness of God in Christ Jesus. Therefore, it is his good pleasure to speak to me. This truth helped me to recognize and acknowledge that I had been hearing God all along.

God revealed that he had been speaking with me from the beginning and that I had not questioned the reality of his voice, even though I did not recognize him. I was hearing his voice clearly until I tried to apply my own efforts to hear him. This frustrated my process, because in an already uphill battle, I had added my fleshly efforts to the equation. Human reason and our ability to figure things out only manage to get in the way, keeping us from hearing God. The pain of frustration, though incredibly strenuous, was necessary to help me clearly understand that my worldly efforts would never be capable of producing a clear pathway to God. They certainly did not afford me an open ear to hear his voice.

In my desperate attempt to hear God with my physical ears only created turmoil.. I had to quiet my mind—my ability to reason things out—and stop trying to figure out the spiritual world in my own strength. Through my own strength, no matter how I viewed it, I only saw a finite, physical, and chaotic world with limited answers. It was flesh.

Hearing the voice of God required silencing everything else in order to listen with my spirit. At the moment I understood that truth, the Holy Spirit came and took up residence within me. His voice moved from the exterior sound around me to an internal voice within me.

Hearing his voice became more evident as he spoke Scripture within my heart regarding the circumstances I was facing. There were many times when his voice began to take on such clarity that it seemed to me like an audible voice coming from the center of my being. At other times it was an inward prompting to do something that sometimes sounded like my own voice.

A great example of this was when I was preparing to share about the Holy Spirit. I was not sure what was happening, as it seemed difficult for me to write down on paper what I was thinking for the purpose of sharing. In the middle of my irritation, I got up and walked outside. I then said, *Lord, this is so hard. I have drawn the conclusion that maybe I should just share something else.*

To my surprise, I heard a voice within me that sounded like my own say, "Do not be dissuaded from this word." Surely there was no mistaking that this was in fact the voice of God. Although it sounded like my voice, the word *dissuaded* was definitely not part of my vocabulary.

When I heard this statement, I immediately went to my library and grabbed a dictionary to decipher what God was saying. Once I discovered the statement's meaning, I knew this was a truth that God wanted to make sure that his people would come to know. Even in the midst of my challenge to get my thoughts down on paper, the Holy Spirit provided the guidance and direction I needed.

God speaks to us in many different ways. As I have grown in discovering the ways he speaks, it has made the hope of hearing his voice a reality for me.

A HEART SET TO OBEY

Any growth and success I have obtained in the Lord was a direct result of God's amazing grace. I entered the process of hearing his voice with a heart set to obey what he speaks. Experiencing transformation in our lives requires much more than just hearing his voice. Obedience to his commands is crucial.

Only by practicing listening to the voice of God and following through with what he has spoken can you come to know his voice. Through practice, you learn what he sounds like and how he speaks to you. This kind of practice will bring about your confidence in hearing him.

While in the learning process, it is important to remember that we have an adversary, the devil. He will attempt to trip us up, causing us to doubt ourselves and God through cycles of distracting questions like "Is it me or is it God?" or "How do I know for sure it's God?" The only result these thoughts ever produced in me was a plague of heaviness and a constant wrestling as I wavered back and forth between doubt and faith.

I learned that when I entertained those questions, I was listening to the wrong voice. Everything in the kingdom of God requires faith. Learning to identify his voice is no different. That single change has been essential in activating my faith.

Now, with this knowledge, I can instantly cast down the negative thoughts and place my trust in God to speak to me and to reveal his truth. This is a process I will never stop practicing. If I have a thought that gives me pause, I don't automatically think that it was just me. I take the time to recognize God speaking. Many of my opportunities for practice occurred in stores while I was shopping.

One day while walking down an aisle of a clothing store, I saw a blouse that had fallen off the rack and was lying on the floor. The blouse was in the way of one of the cart's wheels. I either had to go around it or lift the wheels to get over it. Then came the moment when I was prompted by the voice of God: "Pick it up and hang it back on the rack." Ordinarily I might think this prompting is pointing out the obvious, which is just common sense on my part. Do I ignore this prompting? Every situation, every spoken word, and every prompting from the Lord are opportunities either to identify and obey the voice of God or to be nonresponsive.

"Practice" continues on a daily basis! One day I was in a parking lot at a grocery store. I had just put the food in my car and was going to leave my cart on the curb when the Lord said, "Go put that back by the front door." As I headed back toward the store, the Lord spoke again: "Take that woman's cart with you."

The battle was on! Was I going to obey what I was hearing God say? *Lord!* I exclaimed, *I don't want to ask her about her cart. I'll look stupid! Her cart is still full of bags.* The Lord simply repeated his request: "Take her cart." I debated with myself as to what I should do.

My heart was beating fast at the thought of reaching out to this woman to ask her if I could return her cart for her, although it seems nonsensical to me now to have felt so nervous about talking to someone just to carry out a simple act of kindness. Finally I arrived at the moment of obedience. As I approached her, she was placing her last bag in her car. "Can I take your cart back for you?" I said with a smile. Full of appreciation, she smiled and said, "Oh, thank you!"

Suddenly I felt like I was on top of the world. I had been obedient! I successfully accomplished this seemingly minor task.

This small success revealed something much larger to me. It exposed the large obstacles—my feelings and reasoning—that tried to stand in my way of success. I knew then that if I was going to succeed in all things, I must hear God and be deliberate in trusting him and obeying his words.

Obedience to the voice of God also takes time, faith, and practice. One day I walked into my bedroom and sat on the bed. I began to pray, *Give me ears to hear you and a heart to obey that which you say.* As I continued talking with God, there was this inward prompting for me to stand up. Without breaking my conversation with him, I quickly stood up. I continued to speak, saying, *God, train me up in the knowledge of your voice.* Then I heard his voice as he prompted me by saying, "Sit down!" Without hesitation, I sat down.

Although I began my time with God requesting his help to be obedient when I heard his voice, I gave no thought at that moment that I was carrying out his commands. I just felt like I was simply fulfilling an internal thought.

As time went on, the promptings became small whispers. I would hear, "Stand up," and as I stood up, I would hear, "Now sit down," and I simply obeyed. With each obedient act, the voice of God became clearer in the tiny little whispers. As I continued to obey, the whispers came more frequently. It also seemed as if God was speaking louder.

One morning my prayer time was continually filled with instructions, going something like this:

Father, I praise you.

"Sit down."

God, you are so wonderful.

"Stand up."

Lord, thank you for saving me.

"Sit down."

Jesus, save my family.

"Stand up."

Bless us, Lord. We need you!

"Sit down."

This continued until there was no mistaking his voice. It's different than mine, and I don't hear it with my natural ears. God's voice comes from within.

I was so excited! I completely understood what it meant to hear his voice. In my excitement, I had not thought about what someone might think if they walked into the room. That individual would simply see me silently sitting and standing over and over without apparent reason. I was so elated with God that I simply didn't care how my actions might appear to an onlooker!

HEARING HIS VOICE IN CIRCUMSTANCES

God will speak to us through our circumstances if we are attentive. A great example of this occurred within the first four months after my second encounter with the Lord. I spent all my time reading the Bible so the Lord would teach me what it all meant. After four months of being taught by the Spirit of God, the Lord said to me, "It is now time to go to church." My first thought was, *Where should I go? Where do I even look to find a church? God, what church do you want me to go to?*

As I stood looking out the window asking these questions, I saw the mailman drive down the hill and stop at the mailboxes. I quickly abandoned my questions and headed out of my room to get the mail.

I was surprised when I opened the mailbox and found a small postcard with a church name in bold print across the top of the card. As I read the card, I saw the service times, the location, and a map printed on the invitation. I saw that the church was just a few short blocks from where I was living. With the delivery of that postcard, I trusted that God had just informed me when and where to go to church. I was amazed that God cares so much for me that he would oversee the delivery of the postcard to give me direction. This was indeed God speaking to me through print, letting me know where I should attend church for the first time.

I attended that church for a few months when I found myself at home wanting more. The church I was part of at this point only offered one service a week and a recovery group on Sunday afternoons that I had become part of. This limited number of services left me with an insatiable hunger for more of God's presence and wisdom. Turning on Christian television every day was my only way of filling my time with the Word and the presence of God that I was so desperately seeking.

One day, while overcome by a deep inner need to experience God, I saw a pastor on television who spoke about getting into the presence of God. He said that they were going to be holding a worship concert that would give us the opportunity to be enveloped in God's glorious presence. Oh my—this sounded like heaven speaking to me. I longed for a close encounter with an amazing God.

About that time, my phone rang. When I answered, a friend began to talk about the Lord. I shared with her about a church that had extended an open invitation to the public for a worship concert. She immediately encouraged me to attend. I agreed and made plans to attend. After I hung up, I thought I had better find out where the church was located. My friend called back just a few moments later. She was fully equipped with the time, location, and directions, having called the church to get the information for the concert. We had agreed that we would meet there and share in this opportunity together.

On the designated day, I could hardly wait for the hours to pass. The worship concert was at the forefront of my mind. The time finally arrived. Just as I was getting ready to head out to my car, my friend called and canceled. At that moment I did not care if I had to go alone. It did not matter to me that I would not know anyone. The only thing I could think about was being covered with the presence of God.

Arriving at the church, I walked into the sanctuary, which was filled with hundreds of people. Music softly played in the background. I was profoundly aware that there was something significantly different about this church. I somehow felt the spiritual essence that permeated this church, and it was definitely the love of God. I was hooked.

During the concert, the pastor announced that this church had three services a week to help us grow in Christ. This could not have been more perfect for me. I could go to the other church on Sunday morning and attend a later Sunday morning service and the Wednesday evening service at this church.

I was so excited that I went to this second church every opportunity I had. After the first Sunday morning at this new church, I instantly had an internal war. Everything within me wanted to attend only the second church. However, I felt obligated to attend the first church. At the end of the service at the second church, I decided to ask the pastor to pray for me. As I spoke with him, I conscientiously left the information about my dilemma vague so as not to influence his prayers in any way. I simply stated, "If you could pray for me, I have a decision to make and I'm unsure as to what God wants me to do."

As the pastor agreed to pray for me, he took my hand and held it in his. He said, "Before I pray for you, let me just say this to you: the answer that you are looking for will be in your heart of hearts."

That very second, a moment of clarity came to me like never before. My heart of hearts wanted nothing more than to be right where I was at that moment. I wanted to be part of this church, surrounded by the Spirit of God and the life that came forth out of the Word that was preached.

Although I had asked the pastor to pray for me, it was through his statement that I knew the answer and really felt that prayers were no longer needed. My heart of hearts was saying, "I want to be here!"

Hearing God's voice in that circumstance led me into a time of growth and worship I had not previously known. In time, I learned God's truth, grew spiritually, and was led into a supernatural transformation as the Spirit of God worked within me.

HEARING HIS VOICE THROUGH DREAMS

While learning to hear his voice, there were many times I felt defeated in my challenges. With every endeavor, the enemy presented my failures to me. This constant parade of my failures formed an oppressive wall of heaviness around me that seemed impenetrable. The Lord revealed the schemes of the enemy to me in a dream. Through this dream, God equipped me with information that empowered me to overcome.

The dream opened with me sitting on a sofa in a living room I had never seen before. As I sat there, I was agonizingly aware of my immense feeling of hopelessness. Out of the corner of my eye, I caught a glimpse of something whirling around in circles up on the ceiling. I looked up and saw a storm brewing as dark clouds picked up momentum— as though they were being stirred by an unseen force. I sat staring at the clouds as they gained speed and grew larger until they covered the entire ceiling.

It was then that I noticed a small gap in the lining of the clouds. With each rotation of the clouds, the gap widened until the clouds broke open. Suddenly, as the clouds released their contents, a shower of debris fell from the ceiling. Quickly moving out of the way so as not to be hit by the outpouring, I realized it was not rain or hail falling, but it was a deluge of rubbish being dispensed by the clouds.

When this outpouring of refuse ceased, the room was filled up to my knees. As I sat back down, I was suddenly startled as an old boot hit me as it fell into my lap. I noticed that it was charred in color, as though it had been through a pit of flames. As I looked closely at the trash surrounding me, I could see fragments of discarded waste everywhere, as though I were sitting in the middle of a landfill that had once been set on fire and burned out. Gazing upon all this garbage in amazement, I suddenly woke up.

At that point, the Lord began to reveal the methods of the enemy. He exposed the assignments that had been sent to work against me. The hovering of the dark clouds was the devil's plan to render me powerless, because faith can't be established in the midst of doubt. With each lie rendered, the stirring and the momentum of the clouds increased until I was overwhelmed by the darkness of it all. It was truly by the grace of God that I understood the heaviness I felt.

It was nothing more than rubbish that the enemy had cultivated in my thoughts with each lying whisper: "You can't hear him." "You will never hear because he is not here for you!" "What makes you think you are so special that he would even care?" Instantly my eyes were opened to perceive that my meditations upon these lies that the devil had whispered in my heart were the direct result of this unceasing storm that was stirring inside me.

The Lord also made me very aware of my responsibility to trust him above everything else. This storm would last as long as it would take for me to learn to place him and his Word above the lies. I would also need to trust him above feelings attached to the lie. It was time to fight against every contrary thought and feeling, trusting that if I was asking God to speak, he would be faithful to answer.

HEARING HIS VOICE IN HIS WORD

Through diligence, I began developing my ability to hear God's voice. It was of the utmost importance that I clearly understood how God speaks. Knowing how God speaks ensures accuracy in hearing his voice. I first had to understand that God will never speak contrary to his Word.

Although the Lord had revealed the storm and dark clouds hovering over me, it still took time before I was able to step out from under them. While the fight to obtain my freedom was in full operation, depression continued its vicious pursuit. While trying to fight against the emotional upheaval of it all, I still found myself in a place where I did not care if I got out of bed in the mornings. This trial seemed unending, as depression had taken a nasty hold of my thinking. Every thought was inundated with impossibilities, erasing all hope for probability. *It won't change. It can't be done. It is hopeless, and you are helpless. Where is this God you serve now? If he loves you, then why is he not speaking to you?*

I got to the place where I would stay in my room all day without opening the shades. If the phone rang, I would not answer. I had no desire to speak to anyone. The only time I got up was to go to church. As depression continued in its persistent assault of impossibilities, I was simply going through the motions on autopilot.

One afternoon the phone rang, and I decided to answer it. The caller ID informed me that the caller was a good friend of mine. As I picked up the phone, she began to talk to me about an evangelist who was coming into town for a special meeting that night. She wanted to know if I wanted to go with her. "No," I quickly replied. "I don't feel like going anywhere."

I could tell from her voice that she was disappointed, but I just did not want to go. I was overcome by hopelessness and an incredible weight of sadness. Before she hung up the phone, she said, "Well, just in case you change your mind, it's at this church, and the meeting begins at seven o'clock sharp." Hanging up the phone, I didn't give the meeting another thought.

My thoughts spiraled into a chaotic tailspin. Suddenly an unannounced internal scream ensued as I cried out for help: *God, I need help! Please! I need you to speak to me. Show me what I must do to come out of this.* As these statements were filling my mind, I was compelled to open my Bible. The pages seemed to turn themselves to Romans 12:2: "Do not conform to the pattern of this world, but be transformed by the renewing of your mind."

As I thought about that verse, I wondered what it meant to "renew your mind." As I sat there contemplating, I decided to study the Word and look for the answer. I went into the den and grabbed my dictionary, the encyclopedia, and *Strong's Concordance* off the bookshelf. I was determined to find the meaning.

Investigating the word *renewed* led me to the word *renovate*. The definition of *renovate* spoke of one thing revolving into another thing. Of course, this only left me feeling obligated to search out the word *revolve* until it led me to *revolution*. I wanted to find the answer in its simplest form. Upon finding the definition of "revolution," I was stunned: to have a violent or dramatic change in one's thinking.

Led to believe that I could not hear the voice of God, I hesitated in my insecurity before asking, *God, is this you speaking? Are you telling me to change my thinking? Are you really saying that it requires a violent change on my part? How do I do that?* Instantly I had an inward impression or thought that moved me to get up, get dressed, and get to that church for the meeting that evening.

I didn't think that I had enough time to get ready and get to the church on time, but I decided I would go anyway. I arrived just as the praise and worship was beginning, and I found my friend among the crowd. I took a seat as the people rejoiced in the Lord. They were jumping up and down, excited to be there. My heaviness increased as I watched them worship God with a resounding praise, getting lost in his presence.

After the spirited worship, the pastor took the platform. He was excited about introducing the guest speaker, and he shared a little bit about him. When the pastor finished the introduction, he called the evangelist up to the platform. I watched as this man in the front row slowly rose up out of his seat. Still bent at the waist as he rose, he was suddenly frozen in place. He stood there staring at the floor for what seemed like several minutes. Then he suddenly stood up straight and said, "Yes, Lord. I will do that!"

The evangelist began by saying, "I had a message all prepared for you, but as I was rising up out of my seat, the Lord spoke to me and said, 'I want you to speak on this instead.' Turn with me in your Bibles, if you would, to Romans chapter twelve."

To my amazement, he talked about how he had done an in-depth word study on the word *renewed*. I was floored as he began to explain the route that he took in his study and how it had led him to four different words, ending with the word *revolution*. Then he proclaimed, "*Revolution* means to have a violent or dramatic change in one's thinking." Astonished, my mouth fell wide open. It felt like my jaw hit the floor. I thought, *God, it was you speaking to me as the Bible opened to those pages, wasn't it?*

I found instant peace knowing that the Spirit of God had been speaking and leading me. However, this peace only lasted until the next question rose up within me, doubting God's plans. At that moment I remembered a conversation I had with a woman who had opened an orphanage in the Philippines. She was so anxious to have me come and minster to the children that I agreed to go. Then the peace vanished when I considered my agreement, *God, the opportunity for the Philippines is right in front of me, and I am not even sure if this is what you want me to do. God, please tell me what to do.*

Once again, to my absolute amazement, the evangelist detoured mid-sentence and said, "Let me tell you about my first trip to the Philippines." My mouth opened wide in utter disbelief. I listened intently as he continued speaking: "God is looking for minutemen and women—those men and women who will respond to his call with a resounding 'yes' in a minute's notice." Needless to say, that night I said "Yes!"

HEARING HIS VOICE THROUGH VISIONS

The recovery group at the first church I attended had only met twice, but the leader informed the group that she would not be able to meet with us any longer. She asked me if I would be willing to step in for her and lead the group. Without hesitation, I agreed to do so.

I could hardly wait for the opportunity to share the testimony of my deliverance and make others aware of a supernatural God who desired to set captives free from addiction. The goal for the group was to get them to acknowledge and exalt God as they came to know him as merciful. I was simply ready to help those who would call upon him. My prayer was that each of them would come to know the power of God's Spirit as he broke every chain of bondage that held them in slavery.

One afternoon as the group gathered together, the floor was opened up for any members who wanted to share. As group members communicated their experiences of the previous week, each story made it painfully obvious that the group had become nothing more than a platform for the negative rehearsal of their bondage. As each person spoke, the focus was on the failures—the endless temptations faced every day while settling for a life that would never change. I realized that this continued focus would only lead to their demise in pursuit of true freedom. With their eyes on themselves, these individuals would remain powerless to overcome.

As I sat there listening to their stories, God began to speak to me, and a vision opened up right in front of me. It was as if I was standing in outer space, looking back at the earth. I could see the earth suspended, with the blackness of space serving as its backdrop. With this majestic picture before me, the Lord led me to encourage the group members not to rehearse their bondages and their struggles with drugs, but to focus their eyes on Jesus and rehearse the power of an almighty God who had created all of heaven and earth.

Hearing the voice of God through this vision changed the way we ran the recovery group from that day forward. I was elated as the weeks went on and the stories changed from accounts of struggles to stories of success. I am so thankful and grateful that God would give me the opportunity to share what I knew with them. After twelve very short weeks of meeting together, the group was scheduled for summer break. I knew they would take all that they had learned into their summer. I was confident they would continue their rehearsal of all the possibilities that were opened to them as they remained with God. Their success would be sure as their eyes were fixed on him.

REVEALED TRUTH

The ability to hear the voice of God is one of the greatest gifts that we have been given as born-again believers. Although it requires faith and practice, we are never left to guess what God is saying, because his desire is to speak directly to us. Jesus revealed this as he proclaimed that his sheep would hear his voice and would not follow anyone else (see John 10:1–18).

As I look at the children of Israel, I am amazed that they were struck with fear when it came to hearing the voice of God. They did not want to hear what God had to say to them, so they elected Moses to be the one to hear God's voice. The children of Israel simply wanted Moses to relay to them whatever God said. Adamant in their decision, they promised Moses that they would obey everything God said.

It was unfortunate for the Israelites that they tried to live without hearing God's voice. This missing element made disobedience to God's command inevitable, as the children of Israel only heard the voice of Moses. Without hearing from God for themselves, they quickly forgot that they had been brought out of Egypt for the purpose of establishing their lives in worship to God alone.

In Moses's absence, when he had gone up on the mountain to speak with God, the children of Israel created a golden calf that they could bow down to in worship. After obtaining God's commands, Moses went to give them to the children of Israel. His anger got the best of him as he found the people in direct violation of the first and second commandments. We all must listen for and to the voice of God. This is how we will remember what he says so that we can obediently carry out his wise directives and obtain freedom.

KEYS FOR YOUR FREEDOM

- Know that hearing God's voice is key for your journey to freedom. We must know what he is saying, and we must go where he is leading.

  Today, if you hear his voice, do not harden your hearts as you did in the rebellion. (Hebrews 3:15)

- Trust that if you are asking God to speak, he will be faithful to answer. Never agree with the lying thought that says you can't hear God's voice.

When he has brought out all his own, he goes on ahead of them, and his sheep follow him because they know his voice. But they will never follow a stranger; in fact, they will run from him because they do not recognize a stranger's voice. (John 10:4–5)

I am the way and the truth and the life. (John 14:6)

Chapter 7
FAITH

Now faith is confidence in what we hope for
and assurance about what we do not see.
(Hebrews 11:1)

THE BATTLEFIELD OF FAITH

As I slept one night, my surroundings in a dream were like that of being in a war movie. I was out on a battlefield. The torrential rain made it difficult to see what was in front of me. I was witnessing the devastating results of the heavy artillery that was going off around me while bombs exploded, throwing mud across the sky. I could hear a multitude of semi-automatic rifles being shot off as bullets whizzed past me.

I was down on the ground, crawling underneath the barbed wire to ensure that I kept myself out of the fire zone just above me. As I was crawling through the first battlefield, I could see a trench in the distance. I knew that if I could get to that trench, I would be safe.

Making sure to remain close to the ground, I made my way to the trench, only to find that it was just a ridge to the next battlefield. Again the bombs went off and the bullets flew close by as I headed for the next hill in front of me. I said to myself, *If I can just get to the other side, then I'll be home.*

I crawled on my elbows and stomach, telling myself with each stretch of battleground that home was just on the other side of that hill. Although I was relentlessly faced with a continuous outstretch of one battlefield after another, I continued without stopping, encouraged by the thought that I was almost home. I had no idea upon awakening that this dream would be a significant focal point for me over the next few months. Through this dream, I learned how to operate in faith. Before this, I did not know what faith was, what it looked like, or how it functioned. The battlefield scene was a very accurate depiction of my process of authenticating faith.

FAITH WITH PEANUT BUTTER

Frustration with my inability to comprehend faith became painfully obvious. I was in desperate need of the Lord's help. One night I cried out, *God, Please help me! I keep trying to understand faith, only to be met by confusion!* The Lord was very gracious to me as he met me in a dream in order to explain the principal truth of faith.

The dream began as I was skipping down the sidewalk. The sun was shining. It was a warm day, and I was full of joy. I didn't have a care in the world—until I caught a glimpse of someone standing across the street. I immediately stopped skipping in order to get a better look at this stranger who was watching me. My joy and peace promptly evaporated as I realized this person was no stranger at all. In fact, the individual was someone I knew well from long ago. Immediately, incredibly negative thoughts and feelings from times past surfaced.

Although this was a past situation, all the undesirable emotions were still there. I stood there filled with anger, resentment, and sadness. Then I saw two enormous arms come down from heaven as I was looking up. My perspective was instantly changed as I found myself sitting up in the heavens with Jesus and looking down from his perspective. It was as if I was sitting on the Lord's shoulders. From this position, I could see his arms from mid-bicep down to his fingertips.

Then, out of nowhere, the Lord suddenly had a jar of peanut butter in his left hand. He reached over with his right hand to twist the lid off. As he removed the lid from the jar, a spoon suddenly appeared in his hand, and the lid disappeared.

After being placed back down on the ground, I looked up. I watched the Lord put the spoon into the jar and pull out a heaping spoonful of peanut butter. As he pulled the spoon from the jar, he stretched out his arm and handed the spoon to me. He said, "Eat this peanut butter, and I will heal all your relationships."

My heart's desire was to have my relationships healed and made whole, so without any hesitation, I reached up, grabbed the spoon, and ate. Without delay, I felt every negative feeling, every negative thought, and all the anger that I harbored break off from the inside out. I knew I was free from these hindering emotions, and I began to run down the street with my arms waving in the air! Skipping, jumping, and twirling in circles, I could feel the freedom permeate my being! I was no longer held captive by oppressive memories. I was no longer bound to feelings of anger and bitterness regarding the past. I was no longer a prisoner. I could now enter into my future with every relationship healed and made whole. Then I woke up.

Upon awakening, the Lord said to me, "Yvonne, the peanut butter has nothing to do with me healing your relationships and making them whole. It is the fact that you believed what I told you—that if you ate it, I would heal them. Yvonne, this is faith and this is how it works. Just believe what I have said and act on it. Now, because you believed in your dream and ate the peanut butter, I have healed your relationships."

This was such a revelation for me. I had been tossed back and forth in faith because my emotions constantly conformed to the struggle of my circumstances. Now I understood that focusing on my circumstances will only agitate my emotions, which renders my faith inactive. Through this process, I have become intentional with faith's application to my life. As I read the Bible, I observe God's perspective on any given matter, and I make a conscious choice to believe what he says about the situation.

My desire is to have a foundation of genuine faith in Christ. Although I now know that my feelings and emotions only crowd faith out, learning to set my feelings aside was a separate lesson that was just around the corner.

TRUTH YOU KNOW

With all the incredible things the Lord was teaching me, I began spending more time praying. This journey in prayer created an insatiable thirst within me that could only be quenched by his presence. My time with him made me increasingly aware of his immense love for me. After a year of listening to his voice, obeying his directives, and basking in his love, I thought I trusted the Lord without exception. I thought I was walking in faith.

One morning during my personal devotional time, the Lord said to me, "You are no longer to go by what you feel, but you are to go by what you know." I thought that was exactly what I had been doing. It didn't take very long for me to realize that my faith was still rooted in my feelings. It seemed that the warmth of his presence lifted, causing me to feel as though I had been left sitting there by myself. Instantly I felt disconnected. *God, where did you go?*

Without the ability to comprehend what the Lord was doing at the time, I struggled for months. My relationship with him had been inundated with beautiful experiences, the splendor of his presence, the gentle loving whisper of his voice, and the security of his love washing over me. Now having learned the reality of his love, his presence, and his voice, the time had arrived when I would be required to employ his Word to my life at all times. The intimate treasure of his tangible presence that I had come to know so well lifted.

The battle raged within me to walk in faith by what I knew according to God's Word instead of walking according to my feelings. Being still rooted in my feelings, rather than being focused on living by what I know as the Lord directed me, led to a downward spiral into depression. Thoughts hammered me that I had done something wrong. I wondered what I had done so wrong that God would remove himself from me. Did God still love me? Was what he said to me accurate, or was I delusional?

Confusion darkened my thoughts. Doubts enveloped my feelings. Hopelessness and fear blanketed my dreams. It was the worst time of my life. At times I was so overwhelmed that I felt as if I would not survive. I did not believe I could carry on in the fight because I was no longer sure he was with me. I could not feel his presence. Then one day, suddenly, like a brilliant piercing light from heaven, the words came to me again: "Go by what you know!"

Seeing that light dispels the darkness, I let out a fervent and victorious shout without any tangible proof of his presence other than his Word. I began to pray:

> *I will not quit! Jesus, you said you would never leave me nor forsake me, that you would be with me until the end. Lord, I don't feel your presence, but based on your Word, I know that you are here with me right now, and I know according to your Word that if you are here with me, you also hear me. So, Lord Jesus, I thank you for your faithfulness. I thank you that your Word is true, and I thank you that your presence is here with me now—even if I can't feel it!*

At the same time as those words poured from my mouth, I was elated as the beauty of his presence washed over me like a tsunami. I realized that the doubts, confusions, hopelessness, and fears were the insidious twisted lies of the devil. The demonic enemy was trying to use that same weapon he had used on Adam and Eve to bring the downfall of mankind. The battle was for my downfall, yet God poured out his love on me as I sensed his pleasure at that moment that I had learned to lay my feelings aside and live according to the truth that I knew from God's Word.

TRUST THE FOUNDATION

Although I had victory in the last challenge, establishing my faith continued to be a roller coaster ride with every new challenge. One minute I would trust God and his Word, and the next I would allow a corruptive seed of doubt to cause me to once again question God. When I began to gain ground in this battle, the enemy came at me with different artillery. He whispered, "You are not really saved." These words went off inside me like a bomb. It shook the very foundation of my faith, ceasing all forward motion.

The enemy introduced another lie in his scheme to derail any faith that I had as he whispered, "Is God real?" For the next several weeks, my thoughts were clouded and my faith was unstable as I pondered this question over and over again. It might be easy to assume that I would know the difference in light of my prior experiences, but even though my experiences were powerful, they were never considered in the deceptive moments, for I was consumed with continuous ponderings of what-ifs.

This makes me think of the serpent in the garden as he spoke with Eve: "Did God really say?" God's truth was, "You must not eat from the tree of the knowledge of good and evil, for when you eat from it you will certainly die" (Genesis 2:17). However, Eve began to ponder

Satan's question until it shook her from the foundation of truth—and she ate.

I believe that considering these things one night before I went to bed caused me to have a terrifying dream. The dream began as though it were just another normal day. Suddenly, it felt like I was being constricted, unable to move to the left or to the right. I would try to turn my head in order to look around, but I was unable to move. Then, with a jolt, I was no longer in my body, but I was hovering over it— only to realize that I was lying down instead of standing up.

I was shocked and petrified as I saw myself lying inside a coffin— along with a thick accumulation of oppressive webs that had been attached to the walls of the coffin. The webs stretched inward to form a malicious unforgiving barricade around my head, holding me captive in a dormant position. I was very much alive and able to see, but I was unable to move or speak. I desperately wanted to get loose, but I could not. I did not have the strength to break the dense webs that had been woven around my head.

Then I heard a sound coming from within the coffin. I did not know what it was until I saw some of the webs on the right side of my head break, giving me enough mobility to shake my head from side to side until the webs were completely destroyed. As I bolted out of the coffin in the dream, I also bolted out of my bed. With my heart pounding and my thoughts spinning, I unquestionably understood the meaning of this dream.

God's great love and mercy revealed the intent of the enemy. The webs were all the lies the devil had told me—that I was not saved, that God was not real, that there was no way out for me. These lies left me feeling lifeless and without hope in my pursuit of God. God used this dream to break the strength of the web of lies just enough so that I could gain mobility and fight the good fight of faith until I could get completely free. I knew that the dream was just the beginning of my fight of faith, so I went through the day on high alert.

After I got up, I turned on the television so I could listen to Christian programming as I cleaned the house. My focus was quickly disrupted as I heard a gentleman on the show say, "When the enemy tries to say God does not exist . . ." This promptly got my attention, and I ran into the living room to sit and listen.

As the man continued to speak, I noticed a theatrical set of a bridge set up behind him on the platform that he would use to demonstrate his message. Suddenly, actors dressed as black figures moved out from under the bridge. Some proceeded to crawl all over, while others were busy striking at its foundation. These dark figures (portraying demons) were unified in their assault. Their goal was to weaken the bridge by destroying its foundation.

At that moment, the Holy Spirit used the dream and the depiction of demons pounding away at the foundation of the bridge to reveal the attempts of the enemy to work against my faith. With every accusation against the character and nature of God, Satan tried to weaken my belief in God. With every hit, the enemy was attempting to weaken my faith in the credibility of the cross and the price that Christ paid for my redemption. It was then that I knew that God was not a man who would lie to me, but the devil is the father of lies. With this in mind, I set my faith knowing that I was not trying to get to God, for I was already with him in Christ. I could absolutely trust in this foundation!

TAKE ADVANTAGE

Now equipped with faith, the battles became easier as my eyes were set upon Christ. This did not mean that I never had to fight doubt and unbelief again. The enemy has tried many times since then to get me to question the love, mercy, and character of God. I have learned that he is always looking for an opportunity. The devil tempted Jesus for forty days in the wilderness, and then he left until another opportune time (see Luke 4:1–13).

With this in mind, God supplied me with a key that would set me up for success. It came through the challenge we encountered at the birth of my third grandson, Landon. He was born with a severe birth defect called gastroschisis. All his intestines were outside of his body when he was born, as the skin over his belly was never knitted together.

During the first months of his life, many surgeons and doctors who were working with him told us that he would not survive. I pulled my daughter aside when we heard this for the first time and said, "Baby, I respect the education these men have. I honor the time they have invested to specialize in this field, but they are not the final word. You and I have the Great Physician on our side! Don't accept what they say!" Shortly after this conversation, we began fasting and praying.

It was during this time that I attended a conference in California. While I was in the sanctuary there one morning, the Lord said to me, "Take advantage of every opportunity." Unfortunately, I did not understand what he was telling me. I meditated on it all day to no avail.

The next morning, I got up still thinking about his statement. After another full day of questioning, I asked a friend, "If God told you to take advantage of every opportunity, what would you take that to mean?" He thought for a moment and then said, "I think it would mean to work each opportunity to my advantage."

Although he was so clear in his answer, I still had a difficult time putting the pieces together. When I entered the sanctuary that day to attend the rest of the conference, a video started. On the screen, a man and a woman were shown having a conversation about a chair that was sitting empty in the middle of the room. The woman was telling the man to go ahead and have a seat, while he retorted, "You should have taken advantage of the fact that the chair was empty, and you should have taken it for yourself."

Simultaneously the Lord said to me, "Yvonne, take advantage of every challenge that is sitting in front of you and make it an opportunity to grow and to strengthen your faith." It was at that moment that I began to take full advantage of strengthening my faith in the midst of my prayers for my grandson and in every challenge from that point on. Understanding that faith comes by hearing, and hearing comes by the Word of God (Romans 10:17), I went back to things that God spoke to us about my grandson before he was born. We began reminding God of what he had said about the situation—that my grandson would be a miracle. The more we spoke this truth from our mouths, the more faith rose up inside us.

After months of speaking truth over my grandson, we finally got the good report that he had made a drastic change for the better. His liver was working efficiently, and he was gaining weight. Then we received a great Christmas gift: we were given the report we had been trusting God for—the surgeon was going to release our grandson from the hospital and allow us to take him home for two days for Christmas. After my daughter went through hours of training on all the machines that medicated him, fed him, and monitored all his needs, she was headed home with him.

We were elated to have him home. After Christmas, he went back to the hospital for a short time until we received the greatest report of all: Landon had continued to gain weight and his blood levels were good. His wounds had finally healed and the feeding tube was put in place. Lanny was ready to come home to stay, and we were ready to have him there.

This challenge allowed each of our family members to take advantage of making their faith grow. We celebrated together as we witnessed the complete fulfillment of the miracle God had promised us—the day Landon came home to stay.

REAP THE HARVEST

One day while standing outside the church, I was speaking to one of my very good friends. We began talking about the Word of God. She asked, "How do we do this and receive the most from it?" I began sharing with her that it is how we sow the Word. I told her there had been many times when, unfortunately, I only read God's Word without any further thought on my part. The enemy then stole the Word, the wisdom, and the revelation of the Bible verses I had read. As a result, what I learned in the moment did not remain in my heart. I see this happen at times when I'm searching the Bible regarding a certain situation. I know I have seen a verse about the topic, but I can't recall a single word of the verse I need. This is a perfect example of how the enemy comes to steal the Word of God from my heart.

At other times, after I had read God's Word, a trial would come to directly challenge the Word that had been placed in my heart. However, victory based on the truth of that Scripture passage was unrealized because when the trial got really difficult, I let go of the truth and revelation of that passage. As a result, that section of Scripture didn't produce any fruit in my life.

Then there were those times when I read the Word and it dropped down into my heart. I meditated on it for a while, but eventually got distracted by other things. That Word only produced a small harvest.

Finally, there were those moments when I read the Word, spoke it, meditated on it, believed it, and stood firm on it. I received the hundredfold harvest that the Word speaks about (Matthew 13:23). As I was saying this, I could see it like a movie in front of me. I saw the soil being tilled, with rocks and thorns being meticulously removed from the soil. With great care, the soil was fertilized and watered until all the elements worked together, producing a plentiful harvest when the crops were fully grown.

It was at that moment that the Lord said to me, "You took my Word, you read it, you spoke it, you believed it, and you did it. Thereby you received the full reward of it as you brought your grandson home. This is taking full advantage of every opportunity to make your faith grow. You reaped the full harvest."

IF YOU REFUSE TO QUIT

To conclude the Lord's teaching on faith, I had yet another dream. I was standing outside at the bottom of a staircase. I saw a big white circle that had been painted on the ground. In the middle of the circle was a stake that had been driven into the ground. Right next to the stake was a bowl, and attached to the stake was a chain. A dog was attached to the end of the chain by its collar.

Suddenly a man appeared standing by the circle. It became evident that this man was the dog's master. The dog went running toward his master as the chain extended to the limits of its length. His master stood just outside the edge of this circle and reached out to the dog with a treat in his hand. The dog kept leaning toward his master, pulling against the chain that held him in place, wanting desperately to get his teeth into that treat.

With each pull against the chain, the dog's master would lean in just a little bit more to allow his dog to get closer to reaching the treat and enjoying its flavor. With one more pull, the dog stood up on its back paws in order to lean as far forward as possible. The dog's master was stretching his arm ever so slightly forward to get the dog nearer to getting its teeth into the treat, when all of a sudden, just as the dog had the treat within its bite, the dog gave up. The dog stood on all four paws, casually walked over to the bowl that was next to the stake in the ground, and began to eat from the bowl.

When I awoke, I heard, "Never settle for less than God's best for you." This has helped me many times when my faith wanted to give up. It has helped me to hold fast, knowing that God is standing there with me. With every push I make to reach his best, he is there helping to ensure victory.

It was not long after this event that the Lord spoke to me as I was in my office one day. He said, "Yvonne, if you refuse to quit, you will never fail." I knew that God was saying that if I would continue to press in with my faith, even if I came up short, it would not be failing as long as I would get back up and keep pressing forward. If I would do my part, he would see to it that failure would not happen. What an amazing promise from God!

I also trust that if you will take this promise and present it before the Lord, he will honor his word for you too. This I know for sure. God is no respecter of persons. What he has done for me, he will absolutely do for you.

REVEALED TRUTH

Walking by faith does not come easy. It requires that we must fight in the face of trials and in the face of great spiritual opposition. We must hold fast to God and his Word, knowing that if we will but trust him, he will be faithful.

By observing the children of Israel, we can see the importance of faith for those who belong to God. Faith plays a significant role in obtaining the promises of God. The children of Israel sent out their cries for deliverance to God as they were held slaves to Pharaoh. God then prepared Moses to act and speak on his behalf to Pharaoh, demanding the release of the Israelites. From the moment Moses entered the scene, God had their deliverance in full motion. From the perspective of the Israelites, however, deliverance was nowhere in sight. Their taskmasters, with extreme harshness, forced them to increase their labors.

God wanted to assure the Israelites that he was there to bring them out of their bondage, and he told Moses to go and declare to them that he would in fact deliver them. God wanted them to know that they belonged to him and that he was still their God. God continued his efforts to reassure them as he told Moses to remind them of his covenant promise of Canaan, which was a promise of a better life. The Bible says the Israelites did not listen to Moses because of the anguish and cruel bondage they suffered (Exodus 6:9). It is easy on this side of that story to see God in motion and wonder why the children of Israel would question God's word.

I can recall moments in my past when my trials created an emotional upheaval within me that left me unwilling to go to God's Word because of the anguish within my soul. *Why does God not answer? Why do his promises escape me?* These were the questions I had as I cried out for hours, only to hear the twisted notion that God was hiding himself and was not listening to me. This is where I had to be deliberate in pulling up my spiritual bootstraps as I would scream out, "Yvonne, what do you know? God, I know you are for me! I know you hear me! I know you will never leave me!"

This is where faith must be gathered. The hardest part of mustering faith is understanding that faith is not a feeling. It requires reliance upon truth. Look at the Israelites in Egypt before they experienced their freedom from the tyranny of slavery. We can see in the Bible that God was moving on their behalf to bring them out. What he did for them, he still does for us today as we call on him and use our faith.

Faith is key! By faith, Noah built an ark and was saved. It was by faith that Abram left all he knew to walk with God. It was faith that caused Joshua and Caleb to declare, "We are well able!" There may be times when we face situations and circumstances that would appear to be insurmountable. However, it is because of him that we know that all things are possible (Matthew 19:26). It is because of him that we know that all things work together for our good (Romans 8:28). Nothing shall be impossible to those who believe. This takes faith!

KEYS FOR YOUR TRANSFORMATION

- Understand that faith is not a feeling; it is confidence in Jesus Christ. It is trusting in the price he paid for your freedom.

  Now faith is confidence in what we hope for and assurance about what we do not see. (Hebrews 11:1)

- Know that God is faithful, so come asking in faith. Recognize that doubt is a tactic of the enemy to keep you from inheriting God's promises.

  But let him ask in faith, with no doubting, for the one who doubts is like a wave of the sea that is driven and tossed by the wind. (James 1:6 ESV)

- Remember—if you will refuse to quit, you will never fail!

  Imitate those who through faith and patience inherit what has been promised. (Hebrews 6:12)

Chapter 8
INTIMACY WITH GOD

*One thing I ask from the LORD, this only do
I seek: that I may dwell in the house of the LORD
all the days of my life, to gaze on the beauty of
the LORD and to seek him in his temple.*
(Psalm 27:4)

MY FIRST LOVE

After having had such a supernatural experience with God, I often found myself examining the events that led to my deliverance. I explored every detail, from the moment he walked into my life to the experience of God's gift of salvation and healing. He had brought me out of a vicious addiction that stole eleven and a half years of my life. He made me a new creation, and every time I think of it, I'm completely captivated by him. His love for me sought and found me before I knew him. What could I do but make him my first love? Jesus is everything to me, and sharing my days with him is my highest honor.

After I was born again, one of my greatest pleasures was spending time with my family. I would pray on my way to see them and say, *Lord, if you will open the door of opportunity for me to speak your name,*

I will walk through it. Many times I was greeted with rolling eyes as I would walk through the door, but it didn't matter to me. I knew that if I kept speaking about Jesus, faith would come to them, and I trusted him for their salvation.

One morning I made arrangements to meet my sister at a restaurant for coffee. While she was at the counter placing her order, the Spirit of God moved on me. I began thanking God for the morning and for time spent with my sister, and like any conversation with him, it led to my gratefulness for the life I now had because of what he had done for me. Even four months earlier, I would have never thought this kind of peace and joy could have ever been mine to possess. How do I say thank you for a gift that surpasses anything that I had ever known? Overwhelmed, I simply whispered, *I'm so in love with you, Jesus!* I was elated as he had revealed to me for the first time a genuine love that was unconditional, unfailing, and everlasting.

As my sister approached the table, she smiled and asked, "Are you talking to him again?" Returning the smile, I responded, "Of course!" Then I suddenly thought, *If she saw me from the counter talking to the Lord, how many others in the restaurant were watching me?* It must have looked very odd to them as I sat there alone carrying on a conversation under my breath with tears welling up in my eyes. Quite honestly, I was not concerned about how I might look to anyone else. I was consumed with how I looked to him.

For a year and a half, I devoted myself and my time to seeking his presence. I would often tell him, *I don't want to ask you for anything. I just want to sit here and be with you.* My heart was set on fire, quenched only by his presence. An insatiable hunger rumbled within the depths of my being that only he could satisfy. Perceiving his voice as he would speak and feeling the warmth of his embrace was the highlight of my days.

As wonderful as all this was, I think it is important to mention that I wasn't always in that blissful state. There were many lessons I still needed to learn and many spiritual truths I did not understand as a young believer. I went through several stages in my intimacy with God. My love relationship with God would go through an obstacle course of ups and downs. One minute my eyes would be fixed on Christ, and then, with a faint whisper of accusation, my eyes would turn to myself. I would be inundated by all my shortcomings that seemed to stand like a chasm between me and God. I was ignorant of the schemes and tricks of the enemy. These apparent upheavals in my life would continue until I learned to keep my eyes fixed on him.

Casting accusations is definitely one of the devil's favorite things to do. He paraded images before my face of how awful I was for not reading my Bible for the first hour of my morning. He would cleverly question me, "How could you possibly think that God would care to speak to you? You didn't set time aside to pray for an hour." I think this one might be his favorite: "What makes you think that you have any right to go before God and ask him for anything? That is rather arrogant, don't you think?" It was a continual onslaught as he would point out my every failure.

The unfortunate part of this situation was that I began to look at myself and agree with what the enemy was saying about me. *That's right! I didn't pray or read my Bible for a solid hour. God's not going to speak to me!* The disastrous result of this mindset leads straight to legalism (following the letter of biblical law) and a performance-based relationship with God. This line of thinking regrettably created a chasm in my intimacy with my heavenly Father.

From this apparent place of separation, it seemed hopeless. Would I ever have the intimacy I once enjoyed with the Lord? Although I felt horrible in this particular part of my journey, the

Lord was still working his plan for me. He was still in relentless pursuit of me with his love. There was still much that I had to learn. God was seeing to it that I would gain the knowledge and wisdom I needed, even if it meant allowing me to switch my focus from him to myself. My own decisions would cause me to go through this troubling time. It was more important to God that I was grounded and rooted in his Word. He wanted me to walk with him in faith and fully trust him.

I believe the most difficult part of this journey for me was a result of the praise I received as a child for my accomplishments. As I was growing up, a lot of demands were placed on me to study hard, do my best, and be the best in everything I set out to accomplish. These expectations helped me immensely, as I would receive accolades from the teachers and unceasing applause from my mom and dad. The better I did, the more love and approval I received.

Learning this behavior in my childhood only proved to be harmful as I grew in intimacy with the Lord. Without even realizing it, I was desperately trying to earn God's love. I still thought that if I did better, read longer, and studied harder, then God would love me more. This is far from the truth. This thinking cycle only made me successful in criticizing myself, in finding fault with myself, and in condemning myself. This self-denigrating attitude created a self-crafted chasm between me and God. The result was that it seemed impossible for me to sense his presence, hear his voice, or even believe he was still with me.

CRUISING THE COAST

I was desperate to connect intimately with God and get back what I felt I had lost. I decided to take a class on "true worship" while attending a worship conference. As the class began, the instructor began sharing his version of my life from the pulpit.

He was telling of times when he desperately needed refreshing in his walk with the Lord. He said that he felt he had reached a place where it was difficult to see God because of the weight of his own failures. I remember thinking, *Was he there in the room as I was crying out to God?* The way he viewed himself and the weight of his own failures were dragging him down, making it hard for him to see God at all.

As I sat there awestruck with every word the instructor spoke, I knew I was in the right place at the right time. I didn't realize that God was working his plan for me in his relentless pursuit of me.

The instructor took us to Colossians 3 and said, "I want you to take the next fifteen minutes alone and read this chapter. As you read it, I want you to view it like you were going on a Sunday drive up the coastline. Drive slowly and observe the beauty of the scenery as you go. Stop and rest in order to fully enjoy the breathtaking view."

As I began to read, I wanted to make sure that I moved slowly in order to see all the beauty that was held within the words. I prayed that God would open my eyes to see the splendor contained within each line, beginning with the first verse: "If then you have been raised with Christ, seek the things that are above, where Christ is, seated at the right hand of God" (ESV).

As I read this passage, it felt as if I was being hit with stones of condemnation. It pointed out the very things I felt I was failing miserably in. "Seek the things that are above, where Christ is." All my focus was pointed at my futile attempts to do what this verse was asking me to do. In spite of the incredible amount of guilt I was feeling in that moment, I chose to keep reading.

"Set your minds on things that are above, not on things that are on earth. For you have died, and your life is hidden with Christ in God" (Colossians 3:2–3 ESV). As I continued, the Lord opened the eyes of my understanding, and suddenly, there it was! I was thrilled when I saw it! "For you have died." Now that may not be a statement that most people might rejoice in, but I realized something incredible. I had died, and my life was now "hidden with Christ in God." The truth was now mine as God said, "If you died, why do you keep looking at yourself?" Excited, I wanted to make sure I heard correctly. So I read again, "If then you have been raised with Christ." Eureka! I just struck gold! I realized this is a past tense statement! If I was raised with him, then it must mean that I'm still with him! It does not matter how I feel. What matters most is that I know the truth, and this truth has made me free.

I recognized that the only thing I really needed to do was to "set my mind" on the things above. I immediately perceived that phrase to mean that I needed to focus my attention on being godly. Although this was fact, my understanding was not correct. I thought it meant I was to focus on being holy and righteous. However, thinking this way would only leave me open to fall back into a legalistic mindset.

I took some time to study the phrase "set your minds." I found this phrase meant much more than I thought. The Holy Spirit led the way as he taught me and said:

> Yvonne, setting your mind is like digging your heels in. Set your foot firmly on my Word so that you are not moved. It is much like what you see in a tug-of-war contest. Each side attempts to overpower the other. However, by one side firmly digging their heels into the ground and leaning back, they will be able to pull the other side over. So set your mind. Dig your heels in. You are not trying to be righteous; you are righteous! You are not trying to be holy; you are holy! You are not trying to get to me; you are in me!

This revealed truth changed everything.

DANCE WITH ME

I was in church one day and the music was playing. My eyes were closed and my arms were lifted up in worship. A vision suddenly opened up in front of me. I saw a woman standing in a giant room. Jesus approached her with a smile on his face, and said, "Dance with me." With a slight smile and a nod, she reached out her hand and placed it in his. He gently led her out onto a ballroom floor. With the rhythm of the music, he began to lead her in each step. With her left hand on his shoulder and her right hand in his, her head was turned to the left and tipped down toward the floor.

I discerned that the position of her head was due to her feelings about herself. She was disheartened, causing her head to hang low. Then the Lord led her in a step backward as he stepped forward. With that single step forward, he leaned into her and gently whispered, "I am your champion."

With that statement, her chin came up ever so slightly. With their next step, the Lord leaned in again and whispered, "I am the lover of your soul." Her chin came up a bit higher. Once more he leaned in with another step, saying with the same tender sound, "I am the lifter of your head." Her dance with Jesus lasted for some time, but with each step her head raised, and her chin was now upright. She was in absolute alignment as she maintained each step with him. As he continued to gently whisper, each word seemed to move her until she was flawless in stature and picture-perfect in form.

Instantly, I was back in the sanctuary as the music continued to play. The Lord whispered, "Lean on me and let me lead you. I have already perfected your position in me. You are perfect in form, blameless, forgiven, righteous, and most of all—loved by me." At that moment, I was reassured yet again that God loved me without having placed any conditions of performance on that love. He wanted me to know that his love was unconditional, because he knew that revealing this powerful truth to me would set me free from the lies of Satan. He knew his truth would empower me to walk in confident trust in him. Now I walk through life with my head lifted up, knowing that he has perfected me in himself—and I'm free to rest in this truth.

Just as he whispered to me on that glorious day, so it is written in the Bible for all who will put their faith in him and in the work of his cross. Isaiah 53:5 (NKJV) says, "He was wounded for our transgressions, He was bruised for our iniquities; the chastisement for our peace was upon Him, and by His stripes we are healed." His love for us paid the price for our sin.

He whispered, "Lean on me and let me lead you." Psalm 32:8 (KJV) says, "I will instruct thee and teach thee in the way which thou shalt go: I will guide thee with mine eye." His love for us made a way for constant fellowship.

He whispered, "I have already perfected your position in me." Ephesians 2:5–6 (NKJV) says, "Even when we were dead in trespasses, [God] made us alive together with Christ (by grace you have been saved), and raised us up together, and made us sit together in the heavenly places in Christ Jesus." His love positions us with him.

He whispered, "You are perfect in form." Hebrews 10:14 (NKJV) says, "For by one offering He has perfected forever those who are being sanctified."

God is not looking for performance; he desires relationship. The Lord loves me and gave his all for me. Reflecting on the sacrifice he made leaves me with one conclusion: I will love him with all my heart, soul, mind, and strength (Mark 12:30). This truth liberated me from the snare of working for acceptance. I now have the comforting peace of his Spirit as I understand that genuine intimacy with God is not something that is established by the things I do for him. True intimacy and passion with God is available every day, for he is the one who initiated it for us all: "While we were still sinners, Christ died for us" (Romans 5:8).

FROM LOVE TO PASSION

It will always be my greatest desire to live, walk, and have my being in the constant awareness of God's presence, being filled with passion for him while walking in his love for me. While praying one day, I said, *Lord Jesus, I love you with all my heart. I want my heart to burn for you alone. Father, how do I move into a place of burning passion for you?* He answered, "Yvonne—passion is birthed by intimacy, intimacy is created by love, and love yields itself."

Immediately the Spirit of God reminded me of a picture I had once seen. It was a beautiful painting portraying an intimate moment between a young woman and Jesus. This young woman had come and presented herself before the Lord and was sitting attentively at his feet. She sat there gazing into his eyes, patiently awaiting the words he would speak to her. The picture itself spoke a thousand words as it portrayed this woman, whose eyes never broke from gazing upon his face, yielding herself to Jesus in absolute silence. It was an amazing illustration God used to reveal exactly how to get to a place of passion with him.

Just like the woman in the picture, I knew that I had to come to the Lord yielding myself to him. I would have to wait attentively at his feet, gazing at him while patiently waiting for his address. Completely yielding to him would also require that I keep myself from believing and yielding to lies that the devil had used before to bombard my life. I must remember that the enemy will always try to make another attempt, at another time, to drag me down with his deceptive words.

This maniacal deception kept me from fixing my eyes on Jesus and recognizing his ever-present fellowship. The lies of the enemy were camouflaged within the idea that my performance would determine the measure of closeness I would experience with the Lord. All I have to do from this day forward is to allow my love to yield to my Lord and Savior. My love must yield to him above any thought or feeling that is contrary to his truth. This is the catalyst for creating intimacy with God. When intimacy with God is established, it will birth passion.

FROM THE HEART

I love to worship and sing to the Lord. "We Exalt Thee" quickly became my personal serenade, and I would sit on my bed and envision him in front of me as I sang. With my eyes closed, I could sense the Lord's presence. While singing to him, I would reach out to hold his face in the palm of my hands and just sing to him.

These times of worship quickly became a way of living for me: loving him, spending time with him, and singing to him. One day as I was doing just that, I was overwhelmed with waves of his magnified love. The only thing I wanted to do was wrap my arms around him and hold him as tightly as I could, hoping that my embrace would be able to communicate what my heart desired to say.

Words at that point would have been entirely ineffectual, as they would never have been capable of appropriately communicating the immense love and adoration I have for him. Expressions were futile, but what was in my heart and what poured forth from my heart said it all.

As I sat there on my bed, I folded my left hand up to my chest while covering it with my right hand. Pressing both hands into my chest as hard as I could, I said, *God, I just wish that beyond the words I'm capable of speaking, I could hold you in my arms and tell you how much I love you.* Without a single second of delay, the Lord spoke clearly, saying, "You are! Yvonne, when you wrap your arms around me within your heart, you are doing it in spirit. When you hold my hand in yours from the heart, you do it in spirit. Your love, your relationship, your intimacy with me is all accomplished within the desires of your heart—in spirit and in truth! This is where I commune with you and you commune with me."

With that statement, I knew that nothing could ever separate me from the love of God. When trials try to overwhelm me and the twisted lies of the enemy cause me to question the intimate God I have come to know, I carry in my heart those pleasurable, unforgettable moments with him. Those special times with him become my memorial stones, immediately bringing me right back into the radiant light of his presence.

This revelation has transformed my life of worship. It has taken away the struggle of trying to gain access to an untouchable God. He is no longer an outward God who is so far away that I have to labor just to make contact with him. Instead, he is an intimate God. He has taken up residence in my heart. It is there that I can go and find him so that I may worship him, talk with him, love him, and live a life of communion with him.

This astonishing life is all accomplished from the heart. Knowing and understanding this truth brought an immeasurable peace. I love the Lord my God with all my heart, with all my soul, with all my mind, and with all my strength, and nothing compares to that.

REVEALED TRUTH

The greatest example of an intimate life with God is that of David. As a shepherd boy out in the field with the sheep, David learned of God's love, protection, provision, and care as he observed the sheep in the field while he cared for them. David also saw the parallel between how he cared for the sheep and how God cared for him and his people.

Though David was a shepherd boy, God saw the heart of a man who was passionate about him. Even in the midst of his own failures, David was quick to run to God in repentance, genuinely seeking his forgiveness. God always looks at the heart of each individual.

David loved God with his whole heart. Even as king, he was unashamed to reveal his passion for God as the ark of the covenant was being returned to Israel. David publicly danced in the main thoroughfare before his people in jubilant praise and worship to God. His movements were so intense that he removed his restrictive clothes down to his undergarments in his absolute expression for God. His wife was embarrassed by his dance and tried to disgrace him by belittling his actions as extremely inappropriate for a king. Yet King David was unmoved by those stinging words because he was showing his devout love for God, his Lord and King.

Can it be said that we are men and women after God's own heart? Do we cringe under the weight of public scorn and the opinions of others when we express our intimate love relationship with God? A passionate heart for God can only be reached by yielding to his love.

As you continue growing with God, your love with him will create an intimacy that you will never experience with anyone else. Then, the intimacy you gain in your relationship with God will birth a passion. This becomes a passion that burns bright, like an inner radiant fire, revealing that you, too, are a person after God's heart.

KEYS FOR YOUR FREEDOM

- Know that you are able to love him because he first loved you and drew you to himself.

  The LORD appeared to us in the past, saying: "I have loved you with an everlasting love; I have drawn you with unfailing kindness." (Jeremiah 31:3)

- Know that your continued intimacy with God is key to your continued freedom.

  Because through Christ Jesus the law of the Spirit who gives life has set you free from the law of sin and death. (Romans 8:2)

- Understand that intimacy with God is more than just your words; it is your heart connecting to his.

  As the deer pants for streams of water, so my soul pants for you, my God. (Psalm 42:1)

- Recognize that if you love God, you will yield yourself to him.

  Neither yield ye your members as instruments of unrighteousness unto sin: but yield yourselves unto God. (Romans 6:13 KJV)

Chapter 9
YIELDED

---

*I have been crucified with Christ; it is no longer
I who live, but Christ lives in me; and the life which
I now live in the flesh I live by faith in the Son of
God, who loved me and gave Himself for me.*
(Galatians 2:20 NKJV)

IT'S MORE THAN JUST SALVATION

In order to grow in my personal relationship with Christ, I had to learn to walk with him and yield to the way he would lead me. This is not an easy process, as it required that I lay down my own desires in order to yield to God's desires for me. As the Lord began to teach me his ways, he revealed that although I yielded to him by saying I would give my life to him, I had continued to live the way I always had.

My life was not instantaneously transformed, and all suffering and trouble did not go away simply because I said I was going to give my life to God. Actually, it was because of that statement that the devil brought about many trials. John 10:10 says, "The thief comes only to steal and kill and destroy; I have come that they may have life, and have it to the full." I now know who was at the source of my troubles; unfortunately, back then I thought that my husband, not the devil, was responsible for my unhappiness.

Drug addiction was replaced by a short-lived exchange with alcohol. I would drink nonstop from the time I got up until the time I went to bed. I was very easily influenced by my emotions. I found myself trapped in the enemy's vicious rehearsal of offenses that had taken place over the years. This destructive thought pattern left me making decisions that were not in my best interest. My heart had become hard and filled with bitterness and resentment.

Every morning became more intense. With each diabolical rehearsal of my past, I proceeded to push people—especially my husband—out of my heart. I would speak with total disrespect, having no thought or care for anyone's feelings but my own. I began to isolate myself from my husband, until one day I blindsided him when I announced, "No matter what you say or do, nothing will stop me from divorcing you!"

It was in that second that I heard the Lord say to me, "Yvonne! You are not to leave this man!" I began to cry uncontrollably as my will wanted nothing more than to be free from what I believed was the source of my problems. After standing in the room for an hour overcome by grief, my face stained by uncontrollable tears, I begrudgingly decided to yield to God.

Through this hardship, I learned the glorious benefit of yielding to God and the importance of my obedience. Even though it was coated with resistance, I simply took action to yield to him and obey his command. As I stood in that room, I finally raised my head, looked up, and said, *Okay, God. You want me to stay? I will stay—but just so you know—the only reason I'm staying is because you told me to! That's the only reason!* I believed I had every justified reason for leaving, yet I chose to obey God—even though deep in my heart I did not want to. I began to live with my husband as if we were nothing more than roommates.

No matter how hard my husband tried, I was infuriated by his unrelenting love for me. He would be busy cleaning the house while I was at the store. He would start cooking dinner before I got home. He made sure laundry was done. He was busy fixing things around the house that needed to be repaired. His behavior completely annoyed me. I would think, *What is he trying to do? His actions are not real and genuine!* I had been so deceived during this time that all I could see was what I had made up in my own mind. Just as I was persistent in my stubbornness, God was persistent to do a deep work within my heart.

As I yielded to God, I began to experience an increasing touch of his presence. In his presence, I found peace from the torrential rains of the negativity of my own thoughts. One night God said to me, "Yvonne, I want you to begin praying for your husband." Reluctantly I prayed, *God, if you want him, you can have him. Go ahead and get him and do whatever you want with him.*

I prayed this way for several days—until one night something happened to my heart. As I was praying, my heart suddenly became tender toward my husband. For the first time, I was seeing my husband! My heart instantly filled with grief as tears flowed down my face. *God, touch him and save him! I'm not asking you to do it for me, Lord, but do it for him, that he might be saved and have a relationship with you! Save him, Jesus, and draw him to yourself.*

I began to care deeply for my husband. His eternal destiny became very important to me. My perspective about him changed daily from that point on as I prayed for him. I had arrived at a place where I could say that I loved him as a human being. I have become incredibly aware of the value of my obedience and a willingness to yield to God's desire above my own. He has proven to me that all things are possible if I can trust him and be obedient to him.

God was busy with an ongoing work in my heart. He was softening, molding, and shaping it until I was ready for his next request. While I was praying and spending time in his presence, the Lord said, "Yvonne, now you must love your husband the way you love me." I began to shed tears as I shared with God my inability to love my husband the way I loved him. *But God, you are so good to me; how can I love him like I love you?*

Although I had begun to care for my husband, I still had questions. I continued reasoning with the Lord, giving him an array of reasons why this would be impossible. Finally, I decided to stop giving God excuses. I said, *Lord, if you want me to love him the same way I love you, I need you to do something supernatural in my heart.* After my prayer, I climbed into bed and went to sleep.

The next morning, I was awakened by noise in the kitchen. I could smell the brewing coffee as the aroma danced down the hallway to the bedroom. I looked up at the ceiling thinking, *Oh, the aroma! I want some of that coffee!* With that, I got up and walked down the hallway toward the kitchen.

Little did I know that God was about to transform my heart in a big way. I approached the kitchen and stepped into the doorway to see my husband standing there. His head was down as he was pouring himself a cup of coffee. When I entered the doorway, he raised his head, turned, and looked at me. With that one glance, a title wave of love was unleashed that shook me to my core. With our eyes locked on each other, I was overwhelmed as I was washed over by waves of love. Suddenly I was head over heels in love with this man standing before me.

What happened? Instantly every bitter thought, every hurt, every misunderstanding, and every unkind word mysteriously vanished into thin air. The Spirit of God filled the room with liquid love that washed over me, and all I could see was my husband's faithfulness to stand firm as he waited for me to return to him. Immediately, I found myself completely yielded to the will of God as I abandoned myself and my flesh and surrendered to God's supernatural impartation of love.

At that moment, I was aware of the price Jesus had paid for me, and that made me ask, "Who am I to blame my husband or hold him responsible for anything when Jesus has forgiven me for every wrong I have ever committed?" I immediately relinquished control and yielded to God. I abandoned my own will to take up his, and now I understand that God knows better than I do how everything will work out in the end if I will be yielded to him.

From that day to this one, I find that the grace of God is available to me in my time of need. My husband and I reconciled. Our relationship is restored, and our love is reinforced. I discovered during this process that God has the very best planned for us. If we can abandon ourselves and yield to him, he will take the challenges that look impossible and make them possible.

A transformed life necessitates a diligent effort as my thoughts are being renewed. This is what transforming my actions means. This does not mean that I have arrived and that the work is complete. I know very well that the saving of my soul is a perpetual work. I'm blessed to receive the immeasurable riches of increase as I experience the transforming power of God.

ALWAYS EXAMINE YOURSELF

My girls were now growing and needed more room to spread out. Their friends were with us all the time, and we all needed more space. My husband and I had agreed to start looking for a house. Very excited to get started, I set out the next day. I remained steady in my search for several weeks until I found just the right place. I asked for the papers to be filled out and assured the people that my husband would be in to sign them when they were ready. When the time came, I informed my husband that the papers were ready.

He asked, "What papers?"

"You remember—the papers you told me to have ready for the house if I found the right one. You said you would go in and sign them."

He looked at me and said, "I didn't say that."

"What do you mean you didn't say that? I wouldn't have done all this work if you had not agreed to this." I quickly ran into the other room to complain to the Lord. *I did the work, I searched for just the right house, the papers are ready, and now they won't be signed?*

As I stood there grumbling, the Lord gently asked, "What about you?"

Lord, this is not my fault! I exclaimed in prayer. *I have done what was asked; I didn't go back on my word!* Again, with a gentle voice he asked, "But what about you?" I simply continued my debate in an unceasing effort to prove I was not the offending party. *Lord, you witnessed this agreement. You know it's not my fault. He is being the unreasonable one.*

Once more the Lord asked me, "Yvonne, what about you? What about the way you are behaving right now?"

I stopped, stunned, as the Lord revealed an internal picture of mass amounts of shipwrecked hopes, dreams, and disappointments that had been left abandoned in my heart. I was not angry about the house. This was really about the experienced disappointments of the past that would shout out to dash and demolish the hope of this house. This outburst of anger was merely the unwarranted backlash for other offenses that had not been dealt with over time. For the first time, I recognized the depth of the hidden things that were being held secret within my heart. They held me captive to a barrage of littered feelings of insignificance. Over time, these injurious disappointments had planted a root of bitterness. My outburst was simply its harvest.

Now that the Lord had exposed insignificance and bitterness abiding in the recesses of my heart, what was I going to do? I was faced with two choices. On the one hand I could break free and stop my own reaction to the situation and yield the entire fleet of dashed hopes and dreams to God, or I could buckle and continue to hold on to them and remain captive in the shipwrecked waters of bitterness.

It is not always easy to recognize deep hurts and hurdles that are buried in our hearts. It is equally difficult to be prepared to do something positive about it. However, when the Lord speaks a word to us, it has the potential power to transform us from the inside out. We must be willing to yield ourselves and our issues in exchange for God's will, allowing the process of change to be done. If we yield, he will expose the issues and provide healing solutions.

At the conclusion of this revealing situation, the Lord lovingly taught me another lesson: "In every situation, I want you to examine yourself. Never point your finger at someone else. Point to yourself and ask me, 'Lord, what is it in me that makes me feel like this?'" If I would ask this question, God would divulge the answer that I desperately needed in order to experience true freedom.

THE "I" FACTOR VERSUS THE "ME" FACTOR

Although I had come to appreciate the power of yielding to God, my willing surrender did not minimize the pain of experiencing trials. After being bombarded with one relentless challenge after another, I was overwhelmed with feelings and thoughts of defeat. As the layers of my shipwrecked hopes and dreams were revealed and excavated, I was plagued with discouraging thoughts. *This is too hard. I'm tired of fighting. Why do I have to be the one to say I'm sorry all the time? Why do I have to make all the sacrifices to make things right? Why do I have to be the one to take the high road while others are free to do whatever they want with no consequences for the choices they make?*

To be quite honest, I had more than my share of wrestling matches with these questions. Time and again, I would just feel sorry for myself—until the Lord said to me, "You are no longer to hold on to the 'I' factor that rules over your life. Now you must cling to the 'me' factor."

What? *Lord, "I" and "me" are the same factors.*

Then the Lord explained in detail, "Yvonne, you sit and ask your questions, but you answer them with natural reasoning. You think, 'Why should *I* be the one to say I'm sorry all the time?' You ask, 'Why do *I* have to be the one to make the sacrifices?' These questions are victimizing in nature, and you are *not* a victim of your circumstances. Now you must cling to the 'me' factor."

Lord, please explain this to me. I don't just want to hear what you are saying. I need to understand what you are saying. The Lord began to magnify Bible verses in my spirit. "So far as it depends on [*me*], be at peace with all men" (Romans 12:18 NASB, emphasis added). "Search *me*, O God, and know *my* heart; try *me*, and know *my* anxieties; and see if there is any wicked way in *me*, and lead *me* in the way everlasting" (Psalm 139:23–24 NKJV, emphasis added).

God help *me*. Change *me*.

As I took a good look at these Bible verses, it did not take me long to draw the conclusion that it does not matter what others are doing. What is crucial to my transformation is a heart that cries out to God, "Change *me*! Help *me*! Work in *me*!" It was necessary to take on this mindset to see my life transformed.

THE CHURCH IN THE SAND PIT

One day the Lord said to me, "I'm changing the speech and vision of my church." With no idea what he meant, I began asking a series of questions. I waited for his answers, but there seemed to be none. Then one night I had a dream that brought understanding.

I was sitting in the back of a limousine in the seat behind the driver. Although I was fully aware of a driver steering the limousine, I could not see him. I remember feeling the turns in the road as I leaned from left to right while we traveled the winding roads. Reaching the destination, the limousine came to a stop. As I stepped out of the vehicle, I found myself standing in front of a church that had a magnificent exterior. I was fascinated as I looked closer, realizing that there were small individual stones making up this massive church.

As I stood looking at the church, I caught a glimpse of some mountains that stood behind the church in the distance. I took a step back in order to get a better view. Gazing at the view, I slowly turned in a full circle, realizing that the mountains completely surrounded the church. I kept trying to figure out why each mountain was different in appearance from an ordinary mountain. Continuing to examine the varied forms of these mountains, my eyes suddenly zoomed in on the details of these mountains. It was then that I was made aware that these mountains were not mountains at all; this church was surrounded by mountainous sand hills. This church had been established in the middle of an old sand pit. Who would build a church in the middle of a sandpit?

At that moment I could hear voices coming from within the church. These individuals were preparing for a special performance at the church. I could hear them saying that they had to make sure all their steps were in sync so the performance would look good.

I entered the church and saw a group of people all wearing the same type of outfits: black suit pants with black button-up shirts and yellow ties. This ensemble was accessorized with black fedoras festooned with yellow ribbons around the crown base of the hats just above the brims. These individuals stepped up to the stage, taking their assigned positions. They bowed their heads in unison, placing their right hands on the edge of their hats, gripping the brim. It is there that this dream abruptly ended and I woke up.

I spent days thinking about this dream. Why would anyone build a church in an old sand pit? What was the meaning of this? What did God want me to recognize? I went about my daily routine with these questions circulating through my thoughts. One morning my attention suddenly locked on to the mountainous sand hills. *Wait! What does the sand mean?* I went to get my Bible so I could read the words that Jesus spoke about the sand.

As I continued to ask questions about the sand, the Holy Spirit began to reveal to me the meaning of Jesus's words in Matthew 7:24–27 (NASB):

> *Therefore everyone who hears these words of Mine and acts on them, may be compared to a wise man who built his house on the rock. And the rain fell, and the floods came, and the winds blew and slammed against that house; and yet it did not fall, for it had been founded on the rock. Everyone who hears these words of Mine and does not act on them, will be like a foolish man who built his house on the sand. The rain fell, and the floods came, and the winds blew and slammed against that house; and it fell—and great was its fall.*

I instantly understood the meaning of this dream. I'm one of the individual stones that make up the church. As an individual, it is up to me how I will conduct myself as I live my life. To build my life on the rock means I will take the words of Jesus and be completely yielded to them. I will choose to put them into active force every day. This application brings transformation. It establishes a new way of thinking, thereby producing a new way in which I handle the events of life. That is how to build on the rock Jesus spoke about. Now when life's storms and trials come, my ability to stand in the midst of them is secure.

I was perplexed as to the meaning of the sand. What is the sand? As I pondered this question, I was shaken as the Spirit of God revealed more truth. The sand is my old way of thinking—my old habits and my old attitudes. When I practiced these habits, they would always bring forth my old behaviors. As a child of God and a member of his church, my own way of doing things and thinking must come to an end. It is not enough to merely go to church and continue to live the way I always had. A continued course of "my way" would only offer a great performance devoid of the true transformation I desired. If I held on to my way, refusing his, I would continue to experience failures.

After learning this powerful truth, I purposed in my heart and mind to build my life on the rock of God's Word. I have had to be willing to yield. As a result, his Word has turned my reactions into responses by deliberately renewing my own mind. This has not been just one simple decision. Every day I must choose to put my flesh under subjection to Christ's words, submitting to his will and his ways to ensure that I'm building on the rock. Otherwise my flesh will desire its own way, leaving me building in the sand. How I choose to respond to each challenge of life will determine how my house will stand.

THE HIDDEN THINGS OF THE HEART

Although I was experiencing a transformation, God revealed the need for a deeper transformation in my heart. One night after I fell asleep, I had a dream in which I was standing in a house. I recognized it immediately; it was the same house I had dreamed about that was full of spiders and webs. However, in this dream it was all clean. The webs and spiders were gone, everything was swept, and all the furniture was in its proper place. It was stunning in its décor. The atmosphere was filled with such incredible peace that it left me filled with a sense of security.

As I looked around the room in the dream, I saw a sofa to my left that had a beautiful afghan draped over the back of it. As I walked over to lie down, I thought, *Wow, this place looks beautiful. It definitely does not look like it used to. Now I can just lay back, take a nap, and rest for a while.* When I laid back, I noticed the different colors in the afghan. Each color had been deliberately placed, as together they meticulously formed gorgeous rose patterns within the afghan. It was striking and inviting in its appearance. I just wanted to grab it, wrap up, snuggle, and rest.

As I reached up toward the back of the sofa, I grabbed the afghan and pulled it down over my shoulder as I was lying down. The afghan had been neatly folded in half, so as I laid it on me, I took the corner to unfold it so it would cover me entirely. As the afghan unfolded, my eyes opened wide in shock as I caught sight of baby spiders that were rapidly crawling within it. They had been exposed from their hiding place as the afghan had been opened up. I gasped as I jumped up off the sofa to quickly brush myself off, trying to make sure that none of the spiders were crawling on me.

In a complete panic, I woke up. Then I heard the voice of the Lord as he said to me, "Now I am going deeper after the hidden things of the heart." It astonishes me to know that when God speaks a word to us, he also gives us the ability to understand it, giving us the wisdom to understand something in one minute that may have otherwise taken us years to comprehend. When he spoke, I knew that he was informing me that I was indeed the house in the dream. Once dirty and filled with sin and deception, he had come in and cleansed me from all unrighteousness.

However, it did not occur to me that his statement was initiating a deeper work. He was about to reveal some very unattractive qualities that were hidden deep within my heart. These would be things that were not easily perceived by looking at my outward appearance. When it comes to the matters of the heart, the only one who can really see them is God. That is why David cried out, "Search me, O God, and know my heart: try me, and know my thoughts: And see if there be any wicked way in me, and lead me in the way everlasting" (Psalm 139:23–24 KJV).

As the Holy Spirit reveals hidden things within my heart, it would be so easy to pretend like I have it all together and deny the things he reveals. However, I know that will not profit me. If my heart harbors any anger, bitterness, unforgiveness, or pride, I must always be ready to acknowledge it and be willing to allow him to remove it. That is the definition of surrender. I know this sounds much easier than it truly is. I have spent much time on my knees with tears rolling down my face as I made the choice to surrender the hidden things of my heart to him.

It is astounding how things on the surface can look good while things held quietly inside can be completely out of order. I was saved and had acquired some semblance of peace and comfort only to find a surplus of unseen realities about my character. Then I began to undergo a profound process as God revealed the inward places where surrender was absent.

The pain was excruciating as I could see in detail the unattractiveness of who I was inside. The Lord tilled the soil of my heart, turning it over until it uncovered my character flaws and revealed things about myself that only God could see. His abundant love and continued work exposed pride, doubt, unbelief, selfishness, and a plethora of other things. All of it was extraordinarily painful to see and acknowledge. Although it was excruciating, I'm incredibly thankful that God loves me far too much to allow me to continue in such imperfections.

TAKE MY YOKE

Through my journey with the Lord, there have been so many things that I have obtained because of the amazing care of a loving Father. I can say this now, having a different perspective of the challenges I went through. One thing is for sure—things are always better when we live surrendered to God and allow him to transform us.

I recall a moment when I heard that the Holy Spirit is present to help and teach us. I began to call out to him, *Please teach me and guide me as I learn to live congruently with you.* At that moment, I received an internal picture. I saw the Lord approaching me as he said, "Take my yoke upon you and learn from me, for my yoke is easy and my burden is light." I understood that as I joined myself together with him, he would lead the way, and it would always be my responsibility to follow. I have learned that when I try to lead the way in any situation, my peace vanishes. "Take my yoke upon you, and learn of me; for I am meek and lowly in heart: and ye shall find rest unto your souls. For my yoke is easy, and my burden is light" (Matthew 11:29–30 KJV).

As we learn to surrender, God never points to the things that are wrong. Instead, he lovingly allows circumstances to reveal what is deep inside my heart, giving me the opportunity to see it for myself. Then he gently whispers, asking me a series of questions that lead me to take notice of a change that is needed.

Just as the children of Israel were given opportunities for forty years to see what was in their hearts, I was given my own opportunities. I remember one day when I went to a meeting at church. I arrived early to ensure that I could get a seat in the front of the auditorium, but I was unable to find one. I kept looking around trying to find a place to sit. Unfortunately, there were no chairs available. I could feel the agitation in my heart as I was secretly thinking, *What is this? Why are all the seats reserved? They should have just told everyone it was not an open meeting, and I would not have wasted my time coming.*

Knowing the hidden statement of my heart, the Lord simply asked, "Why are you so upset?" I continued to look for a place to sit, but only grew in my frustration as I felt displaced by the reserved signs. Then the Lord asked, "What is the real problem, Yvonne? Do the signs have you thinking you're unimportant?" In his line of questioning, I became acutely aware that pride had raised its ugly face and made its presence known. The words came flying out of my mouth, "Well, if I'm not important enough for seating, then forget it! I'm leaving!"

It was at that moment to my utter astonishment that the Lord spoke again and gently asked, "Are you really going to allow what is in your heart to keep you from learning the things you need to know?" In repulsion, I saw the hideous face of pride that was living in the hidden recesses of my heart. I was undeniably aware that this moment had the potential to make a tremendous impact on my life. Whether the impact would be positive or negative would be completely up to me based on the decision I would make.

Instantly, I was filled with absolute remorse. *How can I be so prideful as to think that anyone owed me a seat? Am I so important that I would leave because they didn't provide a choice seat for me? Who am I? How is it that I would consider leaving, especially after all that Jesus has done for me?*

Surrendered to God, I humbled myself as I pleaded, *God, forgive me!* These were the only words I could get out of my mouth as the tears of repentance drenched my face. *Father, I will not allow pride to cause me to walk out of here, but I will humble myself, even if it means sitting in the last seat in the farthest corner in the back of this building, if I can but spend another moment in your presence and learn from you.*

This was only the beginning of many areas in which God would expose the hidden pride that was in my heart. Pride is such an unattractive, downright ugly, and grotesque quality. I wanted nothing to do with it. I clearly understood that this meant spending the rest of my life surrendered to God. I would always need to be ready to be obedient to his leading as he worked to transform me from the inside out.

No matter the challenges and emotional storms that loom, I can find security and confidence in the midst of that storm. Christ is my fortress, my strong tower, and my hiding place! In each situation, the Holy Spirit was there leading the way, teaching me to surrender in the most difficult things I walked through. In all of it, I've learned that in him I can find calm in the midst of a storm. In him, I can stretch out my arms in surrender. In him, I can say, *Father, not my will, but yours be done.* In him, I can yield to his transforming work in me. As we yield to him, we can all experience a supernatural transformation!

THE RIGHT THING — THE WRONG WAY

A life of surrender demanded the acknowledgment of some pretty ugly feelings, intentions, and motives that existed within my heart. These unattractive qualities can disguise themselves with excuses, making transformation a difficult process. It is critical to understand that transformation is a lifelong process, not a one-time event! It requires a constant yielding of heart in order to overcome selfish tendencies and desires. There may be times when we find we are devoid of peace and freedom because of hurt feelings, wrong motives, and bad intentions. This can be while we are doing the right thing, but are doing it the wrong way.

Let me share my example of doing the right thing the wrong way. Let me first say that some details and names have been changed to protect identities.

I worked for a local ministry helping with overseas projects, reproducing teaching materials, and fulfilling general office duties. In the process of serving with the ministry, I met a young lady who was attending one of the local events. She was excited about her relationship with the Lord and expressed an eagerness to experience genuine change. I began sharing Bible verses with her that showed that true transformation begins when we stop what we are doing in order to follow Jesus.

For the next several months, we spent a lot of time talking about the Word of God. She eventually began working for the same ministry, and we became friends. One night we decided to attend a special service together. After the service, we sat in the parking lot discussing the message the pastor had preached. I could tell she was uncomfortable discussing it, so I started the car and drove her home.

Strangely, our relationship quickly changed. This young woman stopped talking with me, stopped asking questions about the Bible, and stopped coming over. When I did see her, I noticed disrespectful gestures and a disregard for timely efforts to complete projects, often setting me behind schedule in my responsibilities. I knew I had to say something. Since it was Friday, I made arrangements to meet with her on Monday. She assured me she would be there, and we both left the office for the weekend. While I was driving home, I found myself asking God to help me. I was determined to keep my heart right, not wanting to be angry about the situation.

Monday came, and it was a great morning. I was at peace and was ready to have a productive day—when my phone rang. It was the founder of the ministry. He began by telling me that he had just spoken to the young woman with whom I had been working. I acknowledged his statement with a quick "Yes!" He asked, "Did you ask her to meet with you this morning?" I was taken back by the tone of his voice, but answered yes to his question.

I was shocked as he said, "Yvonne, you can't talk to people in the office like that." I thought, *Did I miss something that he said?* Quite honestly, I didn't hear anything he said right after that, as my head was reeling with questions. I cleared my mind and listened to the rest of what he had to say to me. I felt anxious and desperate to explain why I had asked to meet with her. I could hardly wait for my moment to explain, when suddenly the Lord said to me, "Yvonne, do not defend yourself; don't say a word. If you choose to defend yourself now, you will spend the rest of your life defending yourself. I do not want this for you. Trust me, and I will defend you. Just apologize and ask for forgiveness."

The first thought that came from the outrage and indignation of my flesh was, *What? Forgive me? What did I do wrong?*

With a few stiff twists of the neck and a hard swallow, I managed to utter the words, "I'm sorry. Please forgive me." I was overwhelmed by a floodgate of tears as I did away with my will in order to fasten myself in surrender to God's will. It was not easy to remain silent. My flesh wanted to make sure that everyone knew what really happened.

I desperately wanted to be obedient to God, but I struggled in silence. Finally, I expressed my thoughts to God: *Lord, surely you know that whatever was said was misleading. Why would you ask me not to speak?*

With a still, small voice he repeated, "Do not defend yourself. If you defend yourself now, you will spend the rest of your life defending yourself." I immediately understood that my own defense would be inadequate, but his defense would free me from ever experiencing the need to defend myself in the future. So I chose to trust him.

Even though I made the decision to trust God, his defense felt like it took forever to come around. It's amazing how we look for immediate justice when we face trying circumstances, especially when innocent. We want everyone to know our side of the story before they hear it from anyone else. This is only to ensure they hear the truth, of course; that is, the truth according to our own perspective. We really go to all this trouble simply to find validation and get the backing we feel we have the right to have. Although I was definitely feeling this way, I made the choice that I was going to yield and trust God, surrender to his timing about my defense, and not speak with anyone about the matter.

That may sound admirable, but I spent every moment for the next three months struggling within my own heart. It was a constant fight against every temptation to pick up the reins to defend myself. It required excruciating effort to put my lips on lockdown just to keep from complaining. I had to fight against my old nature, wanting to get even and bash the reputation of others. In the midst of my challenge, my feelings, and my thoughts, the devil made self-defense sound appealing and even justified. However, if I indulged in trying to justify myself, I would miss the greatest opportunity to experience the supernatural transforming work of God in my life.

This was not an easy situation. I had to be diligent, making sure my heart did not become hard and unforgiving. I continuously confessed with my mouth, "I choose to forgive! I will not assign fault! I will not count it against her!" As I pressed in to say and do what was right before the Lord, I would still find myself asking, *Lord, how long before you come to my defense?*

This question was made in weariness as I found myself in a continuous battle. I had to fight against every thought and emotion that would tempt me to speak about it with others. I found myself tired and wanting a reprieve. I finally reached the end of myself, no longer seeking my perceived right to be right. I said, *God, even if no one ever knows the truth, I choose to yield to you.*

It was then that God stepped in and came to my defense. Arriving at work, I was surprised to see a meeting awaiting my arrival. The conversation began with the co-founder of the ministry saying, "There is a dividing line in the ministry, and today it comes down. Yvonne, you go first." Instantly, everything in the room disappeared as I turned to speak to the young woman. Facing her I said, "I don't know what you said, but you lied! You made yourself look innocent and left me in a negative light." With that said, the young woman quickly responded, "Yes, but . . ." Immediately the co-founder interrupted, saying, "You lied to us?" At that point I was asked to leave the room.

Although the Lord was present for my defense and I was being exonerated from false accusations, I found no joy in it. The only joy I had was in the grace God gave me to remain faithful and committed to the process of surrender. A day or two later, the young woman approached me with an apology. With a hug, I offered forgiveness. She asked if we could continue to be friends. I assured her we would. At that moment, I meant every word. Little did I know that my heart was about to be excavated by the Holy Spirit to uncover a grueling offense, one that would take me a while to get free from.

Although the Lord had come to my defense, I found myself reliving the event more than when I was actually in it. Sincere in my efforts to guard my heart, offense had taken up residence. Over and over again, I found myself saying, *Lord, I forgive!*

What was wrong? No matter how many times I confessed it, I couldn't stop the tape from playing over and over again in my mind. Five, six, seven times a day I would have to cast down the imaginations. It started to interfere with my time with the Lord. When I was praying, that recorded offense would begin to play again, causing all the feelings to bubble back up to the surface like an underground spring.

One afternoon I fell to my knees and closed my eyes. I saw in the spirit a snake that slithered up next to me and stopped. At first, I got irritated that it was interrupting my prayers. I turned ever so slightly so I could ignore it. As I turned, the Lord said, "Don't ignore that; address it the minute you see it." So according to his word, I took authority over it and cast it out.

I believed the snake represented the offense, and now that I had cast it out, surely that would be the end of it! I spent the next few days excited as I thought, *I'm finally free!* Then one day while running errands, I ran into the young woman. Everything inside of me wanted to avoid her. This was definitely a telltale sign that unforgiveness was still lurking in my heart. I instantly made a beeline to the opposite side of the room to avoid her. This sparked the destructive cycle of offense rehearsals again until I had reached the end of my rope. I was exhausted by the offense.

Devastated by the constant fight within my imagination, I began to get serious with the Lord about the situation. *Jesus, I have done everything I know to do to forgive. I have confessed forgiveness by faith, and yet I find myself entangled with the theatrical performances in the recesses of my mind.*

As I read the Bible, the Lord, with much love and tender care, began to show me that we are to forgive our brothers and sisters from the heart. Forgiving from the heart is essential since this is where the offense hides in plain sight. Let me explain this just as the Lord explained it to me. As I began to ask the Lord how to forgive from the heart, he said:

> *Yvonne, what you did was right, but how you did it was incorrect. At the moment of offense, you built a wall around your heart to keep unforgiveness out. You said to yourself, It's not that big of a deal; I forgive her. Without admitting the hurt, you trapped the wound inside.*
>
> *In order to obtain healing for any wound, it must first be acknowledged. Then it can be cared for correctly to ensure healing. You did not acknowledge the depth of your hurt, so it was not treated properly to keep from infection. You did the right thing, but you did it the wrong way. Now the wound has become infected because you contaminated it with a barrage of internal conversations of what you wanted to say about the issue. Your only thought was to blast her with your words, wanting to put her in her place and reveal the deception to everyone. In your imaginations against her, you have picked at the heartache and increased the depth and pain of the original wound.*
>
> *If you will acknowledge the wound and how badly it hurt you and then forgive, the wound will be healed at the heart level and the heart will release the offense. That is how you obtain and release forgiveness from the heart.*

I was astonished at the Lord's words. Without delay, I acknowledged the hurt, confessed forgiveness, and released the offense. I felt an incredible sense of peace for the first time since this incident had taken place. Without a moment to waste, the Lord took me by the hand to lead me into a deeper level of yielding and forgiveness. The Lord said, "I want you to go to her tomorrow and ask her to forgive you."

Absolutely mortified and struck with total unbelief, I shouted, "What! Why do I need to ask her to forgive me? I didn't do anything wrong!"

It's astonishing how quickly I forgot about pointing to myself to ask the question, "What is it in me?" I was pointing my finger at me, alright, but only to declare my innocence. I didn't do anything wrong!

One more time he spoke: "You said you would still be a friend! Yvonne, a friend loves at all times. You have not loved. Instead, you have taken enormous efforts to stay away. You want to flee every time you see her. You jump through hoops so you won't have to engage her. You have not been a friend at all."

I was painfully aware of the deceitfulness of my own heart. With every intention of being obedient to God, I went the next morning to repent and ask her for forgiveness. When I saw her, I literally felt like I was going to be ill just knowing I had to ask for forgiveness. Pushing through my emotions, I went ahead and asked, "May I speak to you when you have a minute?"

"Okay," she replied.

As soon as the opportunity to speak with her presented itself, I took a deep breath, my entire being trembling. We sat down, and I began to explain how I had given her my word that I would continue to be a friend. I acknowledged that I had not kept my word, but had in fact withdrawn from her completely. After my explanation, I simply said, "I'm sorry. Will you please forgive me?" As these words came forth from my mouth, I felt God snap the chains of offense off my heart. This was different, and I knew I was completely free. Unforgiveness had been broken, rendered powerless by the power of God.

God loves us so much that he will reveal the hidden things in our hearts, not to condemn us, but in order to bring us his healing power. Jesus will restore us if we will yield ourselves to his will. I believe that is why the Bible says, "Give all your worries and cares to God, for he cares about you" (1 Peter 5:7 NLT).

EMBRACE AND RELEASE

There are two components to living a life yielded to God. First we must be willing to embrace the will of God, and then we must release our own wills, knowing that his intentions toward us are always good. If we truly believe this, then embracing the very concept of surrender is much easier to do.

As we learn to walk yielded to the Lord, we are also required to surrender and release the things that try to hold us captive. These may be things we have not even considered, as they may not have announced their presence to us. Deceitful things like doubt and unbelief whisper and tell us that God is not who he says he is and that he will not do what the Bible says he will do.

I remember sitting in my office one day and reading about the parting of the Red Sea. I was overwhelmed as God Almighty moved on behalf of the children of Israel to provide a way of escape from their enemies. It caused me to stop and ask myself, *How is it that I can doubt God when I see all the miraculous works he performed in the Bible?* Concluding that I didn't know the answer, I decided to ask the one who does! Lifting up my voice, I asked, *God, how can I see the miraculous works of your hand, like when you part the Red Sea, heal the sick, provide food in the wilderness, raise the dead, and cause the lame to walk—and still I question if you will work miraculously for me? Why do I question you? Why do I question your provision?*

I was flabbergasted as the Lord answered all my questions with one statement: "Yvonne, it's because you believe in me, but you don't believe *in* me!" I immediately wept as I clearly understood his statement. He was saying, "Yvonne, you believe that I exist and that I'm with you, but you do not believe in my character. You do not believe that I will do what I say I will do. You do not believe that my nature is that of a loving, caring, faithful Father to you!"

I was filled with grief and joy simultaneously. Joy filled my heart as I caught sight of God's character and nature toward me. As a caring, faithful Father, he will provide for all my needs. Then grief set in as I considered the doubt and unbelief in my heart that interfered with receiving his best. Upon recognizing my doubt and unbelief, I immediately repented and surrendered it all to him.

A life yielded to God trusts in his character and nature, believing *in* him. He is my Father! It is his pure delight to provide for me, to protect me, to keep me, and to care for me!

REVEALED TRUTH

It is often difficult for us to see and acknowledge the things within our hearts that need to be changed. It is always easier to point the finger and blame someone or something else for where we are in our behavior. I realize this truth through my own experience, and it is confirmed as I read about the children of Israel.

Being delivered from Pharaoh and brought out of Egypt, the children of Israel would spend the next forty years traveling by foot through the wilderness. It was during that journey that God began to reveal the hidden things that they had in their hearts as they grumbled and complained against him during their journey. They did not trust in God's character. They did not believe that it was in his nature to do what he said he would do.

With each challenge the children of Israel faced, it was easier for them to point their fingers at Moses and blame him for taking them out of Egypt and to hold him personally responsible for their situation. It was in those moments that God gave an opportunity for the children of Israel to acknowledge what was in their hearts. Full of doubt and unbelief, they failed to recognize that God was their deliverer. Their ability to blame Moses for their circumstances blinded them from seeing that what was in their hearts was the real issue. Unfortunately, their inability to embrace God's will and release their doubts and fears kept them from inheriting all God had promised.

Deuteronomy 8:2 (NKJV) says, "And you shall remember that the LORD your God led you all the way these forty years in the wilderness, to humble you and test you, to know what was in your heart, whether you would keep His commandments or not."

Here we see God leading them in the wilderness to humble and test them and to know what was in their hearts. If we don't understand the character and nature of God, we would view those words from a negative perspective. It would almost sound as if God was trying to prove that the children of Israel were a bunch of faithless sinners. On the contrary! God was trying to get them to recognize their weakness so that he could raise them up in his strength to inherit the promised land.

Do you think God needed to find out what was in their hearts? No, of course not! God already knew, just as he knows what is in our hearts. The children of Israel failed to recognize the condition of their own hearts, causing them to miss out on the promised blessing of God.

May we learn from them and be quick to point our fingers to ourselves and ask the hard question, "God, what is in my heart that makes me feel this way?" Then, if we surrender to him, humble ourselves, and release our doubts and fears, he will raise us up in the promise of abundant life in Christ Jesus.

KEYS FOR YOUR FREEDOM

- Know that yielding to God is more than just receiving salvation. It is also the process of denying self and following Christ.

Then said Jesus to his disciples, "Whoever wants to be my disciple must deny themselves and take up their cross and follow me." (Matthew 16:24)

- Understand that when you face challenges, God always has a bigger purpose—to reveal what is hidden in your heart.

  Remember how the LORD your God led you all the way in the wilderness these forty years, to humble and test you in order to know what was in your heart, whether or not you would keep his commands. (Deuteronomy 8:2)

- Trust that yielding to God will produce good things in your life.

  We know that all things work together for good to those who love God, to those who are the called according to His purpose. (Romans 8:28 NKJV)

Chapter 10
TRIALS, TRANSITIONS, AND CHANGES

---

*Let perseverance finish its work so that you
may be mature and complete,
not lacking anything.*
(James 1:4)

LET GO AND LET GOD

I have faced incredible challenges on my journey that have exposed the working of doubt and unbelief in my heart. This proved the need for me to learn to navigate my way through transitions in order to experience enduring change. Needless to say, the transitions, though difficult, are necessary if we desire the will of God for our lives.

Enduring change always requires renewing the mind. This can prove to be incredibly difficult. Viewing our circumstances through our own perspectives can lead to a skewed looking glass, thus keeping us resistant to change. As I encountered changes and transitions—whether in relationships, at church, or at work—the greatest challenge was learning to let go and let God. God's desire is that I learn to trust his intentions and allow trials to bring me into a place of maturity in my relationship with him.

Maturity and trusting God do not happen overnight. It is a continuous process. Through changes, challenges, and transitions, I'm continuously growing! More times than I can count, I have felt overwhelmed, out of control, and afraid of making wrong choices. Any hope of trust and maturity in my relationship with God appeared to be a very distant reality. I was too focused on my shortcomings, my inadequacies, my inabilities, and my ability to mess things up. Feeling defeated, I asked, *God, how do I navigate my way through trials and know that I will end up in the right place?*

I kept asking with no evident answer until the Lord illuminated my understanding through a dream. As the dream began, I was standing on the ground looking up, watching people go down an enormous water slide. The water quickly carried them to the end. Without climbing the ladder, I suddenly found myself standing at the top of this gigantic water slide next in line to go down.

As I sat down on the slide, the push came and I was on my way. Instantly in motion, I could see holes in the slide, and I was quickly approaching them. Unable to slow my pace, I began to panic. I frantically tried to move my body to get around the holes, as they were large enough for me to slip through. Overwhelmed and knowing I was out of control, I cried out to the Lord, *God, help me; guide me around the holes. Please, Lord, don't allow me to fall through them!*

Instantly it seemed as though a hand took hold of me and steered me through this rapidly moving obstacle course as I continued down the slide. As I was approaching a hole, I would quickly lean back and rest in the water. This allowed the force of the water to keep me in its natural current, which went around the holes. I didn't immediately understand the dream, and I quickly prayed that God would reveal its meaning to me. A few days passed before the interpretation of the dream was put before me.

Sunday morning at church, the pastor was speaking about the trials of change. As I sat listening, the Holy Spirit illuminated a statement the pastor made: "When the road you are on suddenly takes a turn, it doesn't mean you have slipped off course. It simply means you should make an adjustment, let go, and let God have control—and he will direct your course." Now I understood the dream!

This was the key I needed to navigate through trials, transitions, and changes. If I stop struggling and lean back in the water of God's Word, he will carefully move me around the pitfalls of trials, transitions, and changes. Learning to lean on God proved to be a strenuous workout.

I had always lived for myself, always wanting what was best for me. Now that my mindset had been changed, maturity and character had to follow suit. Experiencing enduring changes in my character required a constant examination of self. As the Lord brought my attention to the need for change, I had to make a conscious effort to lean back on him and follow his direction. If I am to become mature, I must never try to justify my thinking or my behavior. I cannot be passive or indifferent either. I must be proactive and intentional about it.

Supernatural transformation does not occur by itself. God does not simply expose the places where changes are needed and then just change them for us. It is a joint effort, a colaboring! The Holy Spirit helps us recognize when and where changes are necessary. Then we must choose the process of transformation, which involves denying self and choosing his will.

I had no idea how problematic this would prove to be as I encountered one of my rockiest roads of trials and transition. My firstborn was entering into young adulthood, making a natural transition into independence. I, on the other hand, found nothing natural about this transition that would force me into a trial for which I was not prepared.

I was incredibly resistant to make the needed adjustments for this turn in the road. I had a difficult time letting go enough to allow my daughter to grow up. Unfortunately, this sparked a series of trials that created chaos, and I did not recognize that I was the source of my problems.

I was the one who was not thinking correctly in the midst of the situation. I shared with the Lord how seriously I took my responsibility of being a mother. I said, *God, you gave me this child to raise and teach about you. I have spent all these years loving her, nurturing her, and caring for her, and now I'm supposed to just take my hands away and allow her to go forward on her own. I don't know how to do that!*

As soon as I shared this with God, he said, "Yvonne, trust what you have sown into her, and trust me with her." I realized that as much as I loved her, God loved her more. With his words, I was sure that these challenges would come to an end. I was so wrong. My challenges were not because of what my daughter was doing, but because I continued with wrong thinking, trying to govern her decisions in order to keep control.

One day at work, after being there for a while, I began having a casual conversation with one of the women there, when she suddenly asked, "So how is your daughter doing?" I jumped right in to express my frustrations! After several minutes of venting, she asked me a very serious question: "Don't you think that you're trying too hard to control her? Can I pray for you?"

Immediately, defense mechanisms wanted to kick in and defend my behavior. As I sat there, though, the Lord made his presence known, and I realized it was truly God who was asking the question. I knew that my decision would determine the outcome.

I could say no to prayer and continue down a destructive course, or I could admit my fault and accept the prayer that I knew I desperately needed.

My daughter and I had always been close, and restoring our relationship was what I wanted most. After my coworker prayed, I left for the day, thrilled with the prospect of an immediate change in my relationship with my daughter. With a new hope, I headed home.

There was definitely a turn for the better as I went out of my way to make the changes I needed. My daughter and I began to spend more time together, and the friction was removed from our relationship. One day, though, I could no longer muster up the strength in my flesh, and the foundation of my willpower began to crack.

Completely frustrated, I decided to get away from the tension of this situation, so I went to visit a different church for a special meeting they were having. As I walked into the meeting and sat down, the only thing I could think of was the combat field that had set itself up again within my home. Completely at my wits' end as how to handle the situation, I asked God to intervene and show me what he wanted me to do.

The meeting began, and the pastor rose to speak. I was surprised as she began to talk about chaos in a relationship. "How do you deal with that?" she asked. This held my attention, and I sat up in my chair in anticipation, eagerly waiting for her to blurt out the answer. As she continued, it seemed as if she had been in my home watching the chaotic events.

Then she asked, "Have you ever been so mad with someone that you just wanted to wrap your hands around their neck and squeeze?" I was thinking that my feelings were certainly being justified! That thought was interrupted as she suddenly changed the tone of her voice, bringing it to a whisper. She was very serious as she addressed the turmoil we can feel in situations that exacerbate our emotions.

She said, "We must always remember what the Word says when we find ourselves in the midst of continuous friction. It says that iron sharpens iron."

Then she asked, "So what do you do in that moment when you are so irritated that you feel like taking someone by the neck? Just stop! You must stop immediately and not permit yourself to stay there, but quickly turn to God."

It did not take long after returning home that I would find myself going back to the words of the pastor. What do you do in that moment? *Just stop!* This echoed through my entire being, and I knew this was my moment to be transformed—but my obedience to truth was crucial.

I began proclaiming, *Thank you, Lord Jesus, for this opportunity to lean back and trust you. Although this time has been filled with friction, I thank you for using it to sharpen me. Just as your Word says, "Iron sharpens iron!" Thank you for loving me so graciously and for leading me around the pitfalls!*

I understood that my willpower would never get me through trials and transitions, but a yielded heart to God would ensure a lasting change. In that moment of surrender, God instantly broke the power of anger, resentment, control, and opposition. It was gone, and I was transformed!

Trials, transitions, and changes have been the vehicles through which God has worked to sharpen and empower me to persevere in relational challenges and grow in personal maturity. Through his persistent care and active presence, my relationships continue to be transformed!

HOLDING ON TO THE FAMILIAR

The biggest temptation in facing change is holding on to the familiar. However, when God has a plan for our lives, there are times when he may need to change the people who have gathered around us in order to usher us in to the life he has planned.

It was just another morning as I prepared to go to work. Standing in front of the mirror brushing my hair, I was contemplating all the things that needed to get done that day. As I finished, I turned to exit the room. Just as I stepped over the threshold from one room to another, the Spirit of God said to me, "Church change." Instantly, fear gripped me and I felt sick to my stomach. I kept thinking, *What? This can't be right! I like my church. They are my family, and they have been part of my life for twenty years now!*

I didn't want to leave. I didn't want to change churches. I just wanted to hold on and stay where I was. I continued in my thoughts until I finally spoke to the Lord about it. I was not prepared to make any change until I knew for sure I had heard from the Lord. Although that was my reasoning for not making the change, I knew with everything in me that it was, in fact, his voice. I knew it well, and this was the plan he had for me. Unfortunately, I wanted to hold on to the familiar.

In a half-hearted attempt to be obedient to God, I decided to go to another church. I knew which church the Lord had in mind, and I headed out in that direction. As I was driving, I asked the Lord to confirm if this was really the church he had chosen for me.

One month earlier, I had a dream that I was with a friend in Spain. I knew we were there ministering the gospel at a local church. After the service, we were walking up a steep hill on the way back to an apartment we had rented. I looked up and admired the buildings as the soft amber light of the sunset caused them to glow with a radiant orange hue. Then I awoke. In the morning, I shared the dream with my friend, and I decided to ask God to open a door for us to go to Spain.

Now, on my first visit to this other church, I walked in and said again, *Lord, just confirm to me if this is the place.* I found a seat and sat down. The music began and the people began to worship God. I closed my eyes, tilted my head back, and whispered, *Lord, if this is the place, let me feel the power of your presence.* I began to worship God and felt absolutely nothing. Of course, this just gave me the opportunity to wrestle with what I had heard.

The worship music ended, and the pastor announced that they had a guest visitor that day. He introduced a missionary who had just come back from Spain. My ears perked up and I sat straight up in my chair, paying very close attention to everything he had to say. I listened to the things they were doing and thought they were doing a great work in spreading the gospel throughout Spain, using the media to accomplish their mission.

I'm sure that many might say that was just a coincidence, but I have come to know that with God things are providential. When he has a plan, he sovereignly orchestrates all the pieces of the equation until the whole of his purpose is lined up. I immediately said, *Okay, Lord. I hear you and know this is where you want me to be.* I was settled in my decision the minute I said okay, and I was fully prepared to make the move.

However, that did not last long. As soon as I was out of the church and driving home, all the questions began again. *What if it was a coincidence? What if God is not calling you to move from where you are? You have been there for a long time now; why would he ask you to move?* This only created confusion and left me being tossed back and forth in my faith. One minute I believed in God's direction, and the next minute I questioned it.

I decided to return the following week to see what God would do during my visit. As I was heading to the church, I began to pray. *Lord, let your presence be there in power! I'm asking that the Holy Spirit would be evident during praise and worship!* I was making my requests known in an effort to ensure God's leading before making a change like this. Worship began, and I prayed again. *God, please confirm your word!* When the worship music stopped, I felt absolutely nothing! I took that lack of feeling and again prayed. *Well, Lord, I'm taking the absence of your presence and power to mean I won't be attending church here after all.*

When the pastor began sharing the Word for the day, I sat there talking with the Lord. Once again, I was inundated with questions that were rolling across my thoughts. I still didn't sense the presence of God, so I was left without confirmation. After the pastor spoke for approximately five minutes, he abruptly stopped and said, "Everyone bow your head and repeat this prayer after me. *Dear Jesus, touch my heart and change my life. Amen!*" As I uttered "amen," the power of God rested on me so strongly that I began to weep uncontrollably. Here was my second confirmation!

One might think that this would be all the confirmation I would need. Well, that was far from the truth for me. I continued to wrestle with the change, wanting to hold on to the familiar. I knew everyone at my church, even with a constant change of faces. I was comfortable in my role there.

Then I began to realize that maybe that was the problem—I was comfortable! After struggling over God's intentions for a month, I entered my church one Sunday morning and walked straight back to the prayer room in order to pray before the service. On my way back to the room, my phone rang. I answered it and began a conversation with my friend. I told her about the struggle I had been going through. Then words came straight out of my mouth that I knew were not my own. I said, "I almost feel like God is saying, 'How many times will you ask me to confirm what I have already shown you?'"

With that statement, I felt a conviction in my heart. The music began in the sanctuary, and I ran out for the worship service and took my place on the platform. As I began singing, I found it difficult to worship. As the second song began, I purposed to engage my heart and sing to the Lord as if he were standing right in front of me.

I was attentive to each word as we sang the chorus to "Forever Reign." As we sang, "Oh, I'm running to your arms," the Lord immediately opened up a vision, and I saw myself run into the arms of Jesus. This brought a smile to my face—until we sang the next words: "My heart will sing no other name—Jesus!" As these words came out of my mouth, the Spirit of God spoke to me audibly, saying, "If you remain here, your heart will be singing 'Pastor'!"

I was devastated to think my heart would sing any name but Jesus! He had done so much for me! Why would I try to convince myself that I didn't hear the voice of God correctly? I had been hearing his voice from the beginning, and I knew it was him the minute he spoke the words. I just wanted to remain with the familiar.

It was then that the Lord revealed my position. Although I met new people every week, I still had the same people in close proximity to me all the time. I had created an amazing comfort zone for myself. I didn't want to step out and start something new. I didn't want to build new relationships. Where would I fit in? In spite of insecurity in the unknown, I was ready to let go of the familiar and move forward with God.

STEPPING INTO THE UNKNOWN

In every transition there is an element of the unknown. The anticipation of not knowing what's around the corner is a frightening thought. God does not show us everything at once.

If he did and we were able to see the challenges we would have to walk through, we would run away. That is exactly what God revealed in Exodus 13:17 (NKJV): "Then it came to pass, when Pharaoh had let the people go, that God did not lead them by way of the land of the Philistines, although that was near; for God said, 'Lest perhaps the people change their minds when they see war, and return to Egypt.'"

In order to grow in God and walk in the fullness of his plan, we must be willing to make the transitions needed. It may require that we face and fight some spiritual enemies to our growth, such as fear and failure. However, I have found that the key to fulfilling God's plan is never to look back to what was, but to keep moving forward with him. I didn't know the people I would meet in the transition. I didn't know what life would look like. I didn't have a clue what I would do once I arrived. However, this one thing I knew for sure: God said, "Go!" So I started moving forward to make the transition.

It was tempting to stop and turn back to the familiar whenever I felt the anxiety of the unknown. However, he had assured me by saying, "Yvonne, if you will refuse to quit, you will never fail!" With his promise of victory, I began to fight against the fear of the unknown, allowing my heart and mind to be transformed by the Spirit of God and his Word!

THE CATAPULT

One morning as I sat on my living room sofa, a vision opened up before me. I saw a massive catapult that stood two stories high. I did not understand why I was seeing this, but I continued to watch. The vision zoomed in on the arm of this massive catapult. As I looked into its cradle, I saw something lying in the center of it. That "something" was so small in comparison to the catapult's cradle that I could not identify the contents.

Without anyone manning the catapult, the arm swung backward, preparing to launch its artillery. When the arm of the catapult was released, I was shocked to see the silhouette of a woman flying through the air as she was thrust from the cradle of the catapult. I continued to observe her as she leaned back in the middle of her flight. She began to swing her arms and her feet to keep her body upright as she sailed through the sky.

Upon impact, she forcefully landed on her hands and knees in the middle of a massive desert. While the catapult had delivered her into the unknown, there was no hesitation in her movement as she set out in search of something. While remaining on her hands and knees, the woman began feverishly brushing through the sand. It was obvious she was looking for something buried by its grains.

Although she was delayed in finding what she was looking for, she continued crawling across the desert floor in a forward motion, scouting as much territory as she could. Her hands moved swiftly as the look of desperation on her face grew; she was not unearthing the treasure she was looking for. With her hands moving as fast as they possibly could, she abruptly came to a halt.

Suddenly a smile appeared on her lips, revealing that she had found what she was looking for. Her joy became evident as she picked something up out of the sand with her right hand while carefully cupping it with her left hand to protect it. While remaining on her knees, her expression of joy increased as she continued to gaze at the treasure she had found.

I sat there wondering what she had found and what she was holding in her hand. What could possibly give her joy and cause her to smile after being catapulted into the middle of an unknown desert all alone?

The vision suddenly shifted in its perspective. I was standing behind the woman looking over her shoulder as she continued to cup her hands together to protect her newfound treasure. Then I saw what she held in her hand. She was holding one single blade of green grass in her right hand between her thumb and index finger, which she was carefully protecting with her left hand. This single blade of grass seemed to give her incredible joy. Then the vision was closed.

Immediately upon the end of this vision, the Holy Spirit spoke and asked me a very thought-provoking question: "If you were catapulted into an unknown desert, could you find one good and living thing there?" I sat there numbed by the question. I found myself responding, *Lord, I hope I would be able to find one good living thing.* I was so perplexed by this question that I thought about it over and over again.

The more I thought about it, the more confident I felt that I would be able to find something good and living. I began to encourage others with this vision—that when unexpected things happen and you are traveling through situations that leave you unsure of what to do, look for that one good thing in the middle of it. Little did I know that the question the Lord had asked me would be a catalyst to prepare me to deal with the catapult that was just around the corner.

Three days after this vision, everything in my life as I knew it instantly changed. With one bad decision made by someone else, my life was suddenly and completely turned upside down. I found myself in the middle of a massive desert as someone I loved had lost control and, unfortunately, was forcefully removed from my life without warning.

The next thing I knew, I was on my own with no one to turn to and no idea what I was to do next. With tears flooding my face and my heart surrounded by grief, pain, and sorrow, I thought, *Oh God, what happened? What do I do?* Immediately I heard the Spirit of God as he repeated the words from the vision: "If you were catapulted into an unknown desert, could you find one good and living thing there?"

I sat there motionless for a while, and then I prayed:

Lord, I can't find anything good in the midst of this, except that you are the living God and you have promised that all things would work together for my good. Father, you are not a man that you would lie to me. So although I'm in this desert facing the unknown, there is one thing I do know! I know you, and because you said it, I know that something good must come out of this! You are my one good and living thing, and I will hold on to you as you lead me through this wilderness.

Finding a sense of peace with the knowledge that God is in control of my unknown, I began to ask him for each step I would need to take through this journey. One step at a time, the Lord gave me his direction. His constant presence and guiding hand kept me calm and assured of the good that would come out of this situation. With each new element in front of me, I would ask, *Lord, what should I do now?* He was always faithful to answer!

The Lord revealed to me the person with whom I would need to speak in order to begin taking the necessary steps to get out of this desert terrain. Without hesitation, I made the call. I was so thankful that God knew what I needed and was completely ready and willing to walk with me as I set out to move forward and make my way through the wilderness.

After a long conversation, I was given steps to begin the arduous process of hiking my way out of this desert. I had been informed that it would take some time before there would be any kind of positive change. Over the next several months, I made my journey down the unknown path of transition and change. One sand dune after another,

I kept moving forward, keeping my eyes on the one true and living God who would lead me out.

No matter how hopeless it looked at times, I knew God was walking with me. I had his promise of restoration and a recovery of all that had been lost. So by daily yielding to the Lord's direction and by his amazing grace that gave me strength, I made my trek. For nine long and precarious months, the Lord worked in the situation—but the real work was needed in my own heart. It took painstaking conversations with him to bring about true forgiveness, and it took a long constant working to renew my mind to the possibilities of hope for a better tomorrow.

I have learned that although transitions are difficult, they are not impossible. I lean on God and depend on him to guide and navigate my way through them. My success is always dependent on my ability to trust that God is truly working all things together for my good. This trust empowers me to embrace transitions. I understand that it produces the fruit of faith, peace, patience, and lasting change.

DO YOU WANT FAIR?

As I was growing up, there were many times when I would say, "That's not fair!" I remember my dad responding, "Life is not always fair." After hearing me say that for years, my dad one day replied, "I don't want to hear you say 'That's not fair' again."

From that day forward, those words were not used in my communication. There were occasions when my own children would disagree and two of them would want to play with the same thing. Inevitably the arguments would commence, and I would hear one of them scream, "That's not fair!"

Upon hearing this, I would jump to attention, as those words had become unacceptable to me. Then, as I addressed my children, I would hear coming from my own mouth, "Life's not always fair. Learn to compromise with one another, share, and get along."

I had learned that things would happen in life that I could not control and that things would not always be fair. Instead of getting angry or having a pity party for myself, I simply tried to move forward. I thought I had a pretty good handle on it until I became brutally aware of how far I still needed to go.

This became more obvious as I received an unexpected visit from a friend one day. I was in my office completing the workday and getting ready to head home. I stepped out the office door and was met by someone who was very dear to me. Greeting him with a smile, I was completely stunned as he released a bombardment of obscenities at me that threw me into utter confusion.

What in the world could he be so upset about? I desperately began to search my mind. Had I done or said something recently that had obviously offended him? Without ever saying why he was angry or what had caused him to have become so upset, he simply turned and stomped off.

Shaken by the events that had taken place, I unlocked my office door and went back inside. As I closed the door and locked it behind me, I instantly fell to my knees and cried out to God with tears flowing down my cheeks. My first thought was, *God, this is not fair!* I felt an instant repugnance by the words "not fair," so I canceled them out of my thoughts and continued with, *Lord, I deserve better than this.*

As soon as those words came out of my mouth, I was surprised by the Lord's response. He asked me, "Do you want fair—or do you want to look like me?" Instantly, everything inside me screamed out, "No! I do not want fair!"

The second the Lord asked me this question, I unmistakably heard what was not spoken, and I understood what God was asking me. I knew that if I had answered yes after he asked me if I wanted what was fair, he would have given it to me. However, I also understood that if I said yes to what was fair, I would be surrendering the opportunity to look like him.

Making any choice that would keep me from being a genuine reflection of him was completely unacceptable to me. However, choosing to look like him did not do away with my sorrow and hurt feelings.

A line of inquiry quickly began on my part as I asked the Lord in utter anguish, *Jesus, how did you walk through this life without ever getting your feelings hurt?* He replied so quickly that it surprised me. He said, "Yvonne, my feelings got hurt all the time."

Spontaneously I asked, *Then how did you handle it?*

He quickly replied, "I gave it to my Father."

But Lord, how did you do that?

He said, "I gave my heart to my Father to care for."

I immediately took my hands and reached up as if to grab my heart right out of my chest. Once I had it in the palm of my hands, I stretched out my arms with my hands cupped, lifting my heart up to heaven. Then I said, *Lord, please take my heart and care for it as if it were your own. Take away all the hurt and the sorrow.* Supernaturally, I felt the Lord remove the burden as he touched me and removed all the hurt from my heart. I was as overwhelmed by the faithfulness of God as I was with the initial encounter of my friend's obscenities.

During the next two days, I thought about the conversation I had with the Lord and the answers he had given me. The next morning during my devotional time I begin to read 1 Peter. There, in big bold print, were the answers the Lord had given me. I was astonished as I read, "To this you were called, because Christ suffered for you, leaving you an example, that you should follow in his steps. 'He committed no sin, and no deceit was found in his mouth.' When they hurled their insults at him, he did not retaliate; when he suffered, he made no threats. Instead, he entrusted himself to him who judges justly" (1 Peter 2:21–23).

I once heard that the answers to every question we might have could be found in the Bible. I thank God for that day, as I felt the victory. The hurt had been removed, the burden destroyed, and he had made me more than a conqueror! There is victory in living a life yielded to Christ Jesus!

GEMSTONES

In all the trials, transitions, and changes I have walked through, God has had a plan. His plan was to use each challenge to stretch my faith, strengthen my character, and draw me closer to him.

One night in a dream, the Lord revealed how his plan would work. I dreamed I was walking down a crowded street. There was a huge outdoor party going on. A multitude of people filled the streets as they moved about. The overwhelming shrills of laughter were deafening as they ricocheted off the buildings, echoing through the corridors of the streets.

As I was watching people pass by, it seemed as though they were so involved in the things going on around them that they didn't realize that they were twisting their ankles. They didn't notice that they were stumbling. Suddenly the people began to disappear from the party. The overwhelming sound of laughter that was once echoing off the sides of the buildings quickly died down to a very dull rumble until it faded away with the people.

The streets that were recently littered with people celebrating were suddenly barren and nearly empty. Where had everyone gone? Why did they leave so quickly? The celebration was abruptly abandoned and the place was quickly deserted.

As I continued to move up the street, I noticed that I was approaching an intersection. As I got closer, I became shaky as my ankles wobbled under the stress of awkward steps. I glanced at the ground and noticed that the street I had been walking on was now a dirt road, littered with stones of various shapes and sizes. These rocks made it difficult to firmly set my feet and walk on solid ground.

As I carefully continued walking down the road, I began to pick up my pace. I continued to take notice of each stone. Paying close attention to the placement of my feet with each step, I made sure to avoid stumbling. While looking at the ground as I stepped, I noticed that the rocks had an odd shimmer to them. I peered at the stones and realized that they were different colors. Some shimmered white in the light of the day, while others had a yellowish tint to them. I continued to study the stones because there was something peculiar about them. The more I looked at the stones, the more color I noticed in them. As I looked back down to the ground, I realized that these were not ordinary stones. They were all gemstones!

I looked up the road and saw a large stone in the distance. It was larger than any other stone on the dirt road, and I began to run toward it. The closer I got to the stone, the brighter it sparkled with a green glimmer. I quickly scooped it up and began to examine it, taking note of each detail. It was a giant emerald! Realizing that it was an emerald, I studied the cut. I could see the prisms and clearly view all the different angles within the stone itself. I stood there in awe, admiring its beauty. I thought this was the most amazing gem I had ever seen! With that, I woke up.

As my eyes opened, the Lord said to me, "Those things that are stumbling stones to others will be as gems to you." At that moment, the Lord gave me complete understanding of the dream. I instantly knew that the people in the dream who were celebrating, laughing, and full of joy were those who rejoiced in the Lord and were celebrating that they were saved.

The stones in my dream upon which I had been stepping that were making me unstable represented offenses that caused people to stumble.

As their stumbling increased, their rejoicing and celebration slowly faded away. I understood by the Spirit of God that each opportunity of offense I encounter carries with it the potential of producing beauty or distortion as supplied by my viewpoint.

If I allow my perspective to be distorted by offense, then the offense becomes my stumbling stone. However, if I keep my perspective anchored in Christ Jesus, then the offense proves to be a gemstone and it becomes my stepping-stone—a treasure of great beauty that can take me a step up in my relationship with Jesus.

Though God does not initiate my struggles, I have definitely learned that he will certainly use them for my benefit. If I know and trust that *all things* work together for my good, then every stumbling stone of heartache, heartbreak, pain, sorrow, suffering, and offense can be turned into an emerald stepping-stone as my faith increases, my character is strengthened, and I am transformed—being conformed into his image.

CONSUMING FIRE OF GOD

In my pursuit of fellowship with God, I spent time in prayer with a friend one night. There came a moment that evening when the Spirit of God moved on her. She began to speak to me about the plans God had for me. Her words did not surprise me, for they only confirmed what God had spoken to me. However, it did shake me a bit when she said that along with those plans, more transitions and changes were to come.

She began to pray that the consuming fire of God would burn away everything in me that was not of him so that I would be able to stand firm in all he was calling me to. After she had finished appealing to the Lord on my behalf, she wrote down the prayer that she had spoken over me. She gave me instructions to pray this word over myself out loud every day. Eager to grow and move forward in the Lord, I couldn't wait to get alone with the Lord and pray this prayer over myself.

The next morning after I woke up, I reached for the prayer my friend had written down, sat up on my bed, and began to pray the prayer out loud over myself. To my surprise, when I reached the line about the consuming fire of God, the words would not come out of my mouth. Something would not permit me to speak it, and I began to tremble at the thought of the fire of God.

For several days I tried to speak the entire prayer over myself, only to stop short, not being able to ask God to allow his consuming fire to devour everything in me that was not of him. With one failed attempt after another, I decided in a moment of defeat to put the prayer away and not pray it again. Little did I know that God had other plans in store for me regarding that written prayer.

One night I had a dream that I was standing in a hotel room with my mom. Suddenly one wall of the room changed, and I could see through it as it became transparent. I could see an enormous fire in the distance that seemed to fill the entire horizon. From as far left to as far right as I could see, the entire sky was full of flames. I stood there watching as the flames began to progress toward the hotel we were in.

The fire rushed toward us as I continued watching. Suddenly I could see the individual flames as they rolled about interweaving with each other. The flames were violent in their movement as they rolled forward to consume whatever was in its path. I stood watching until I realized that the room we were standing in was about to be devoured by the fire. Desperate to keep away from its consuming flames, I ran to the far side of the bed, pulled the mattress off, and stood it on its end to create a rampart that would cover me and my mom. As the flames rolled into the room with a violent blast, they flew around the edges of the bed, keeping us safe from its burn.

As the flames in my dream rushed up around the mattress, I woke up in a panic. I was terrified to think that the flames were so close to consuming us. I did not equate the dream of the consuming fire to the written prayer that I had put away until much later.

A few weeks later, I headed for a conference in California. One morning while we were all together in the sanctuary, a stunning array of harmonies struck the atmosphere as the voices of six thousand people opened their mouths in song to worship God Almighty. I stood there with my eyes closed, lost in the presence of God.

Suddenly I envisioned a massive wall of fire coming down from the far left corner of the sanctuary. In absolute terror, I quickly opened my eyes and gasped for air. The Lord spoke to me at that moment, saying, "There is a part of you that is afraid of this part of me." I was mortified to think that anything in me would be fearful of God. The Lord gave me a revelation of his fire as he continued to speak: "Yvonne, you think that if you submit yourself to my consuming fire you will be destroyed. Your natural understanding draws the conclusion that if you are exposed to the fire of my Spirit, you will cease to exist. What you must understand is that the fire of my Spirit will do away with the things that bind you and will bring forth the real you that I have purposed you to be."

My face filled with tears of repentance as I asked God to do a work in me. This would be a continuous work until I finally realized the value of the fire of his Spirit. This revelation came as I was sitting on my living room sofa with two of my friends. We began to worship God in preparation for prayer. It was during the worship that the Lord directed my moves through different visions.

I was sitting on the sofa when suddenly I saw myself get off the sofa and sit on the floor. When I saw this vision, I did not move to the floor, but I remained where I was. The same vision opened up before me again as I watched myself slide off the sofa and onto the floor. The second time I saw it, I moved and sat down on the floor.

Then I saw myself raise my hands in worship, and again I did nothing in response to the vision. When I saw it a second time, I quickly raised my hands to worship him. I saw one more vision as I watched myself lay out on the floor before him in constant unbroken worship. One might think that I would move the first time on this third round of visions, but I did not.

The minute I did move and sprawl out on the floor, though, the Lord said to me, "Yvonne, every time you hesitate to move when I show you something, it is because of pride. You think you know better than I when you do not respond immediately." I then said, *Lord, annihilate it! Let the consuming fire of your Spirit burn pride right out of me! I do not want it to control or hinder me from stepping into all that you have for me and keep me from becoming the person you have created me to be!* With that last word from my mouth, I understood the cleansing, purifying fire of God's Spirit.

I will no longer be held captive, afraid that I will cease to exist as I know myself. I will securely embrace the perfecting work of God's Spirit as he brings forth the real me according to his purpose—transformed!

REVEALED TRUTH

Transformation and lasting change is a continuous lifelong process. They does not happen overnight and are not completed with one incident. The process of lasting change is only initiated with an event.

God has an amazing plan for our lives, and he fully understands what it will require to get us into that plan. He will providentially orchestrate our steps to lead us to his desired outcome for our lives.

Gideon is a great example of the process of transformation and lasting change. We are introduced to Gideon as he sat in the winepress hiding from the Midianites. The angel of the Lord appeared and spoke to him regarding the plans that God had for him.

Gideon was not very quick to agree with God's plan, as he could not see in himself what God saw in him. Gideon's process of transformation began in the way he thought about himself. Then he had to be transformed in regard to what he thought about God. In Judges 6:13 we read that Gideon questioned if God was really with them: "If the LORD is with us, why has all this happened to us?" It is easy to have this kind of mindset when things around us are troubled. We might wonder if God is even with us.

The angel of the Lord then revealed Gideon's potential as seen by God. God had destined him to be victorious when he proclaimed, "The LORD is with you, you mighty man of valor!" (Judges 6:12 NKJV). God continued to reveal his plan for Gideon's life as he told him, "Go in this might of yours, and you shall save Israel from the hand of the Midianites" (Judges 6:14 NKJV).

At that word, you would think that Gideon would be assured of God's presence with him, but he wasn't. Gideon once again argued based upon his own perspective of himself as he pointed out all his character flaws. The Lord then revealed that he would be with Gideon to bring about a transformation within him and in his circumstances.

God prevailed as he assured Gideon that he would remain with him. God fulfilled his plan and kept his word as he transformed Gideon into the warrior who saved all of Israel from the hand of the Midianites.

KEYS FOR YOUR FREEDOM

- Know that lasting change and transformations are not one-time events, but this is a continuous lifelong process. So don't give up!

  He tells us everything over and over—one line at a time, one line at a time, a little here, and a little there! (Isaiah 28:10 NLT)

- Understand that when you yield to God, he will lead you and give you counsel.

  I will instruct you and teach you in the way you should go;
  I will counsel you with my loving eye on you. (Psalm 32:8)

- Trust that when God calls you into the unknown, he will keep you secure.

  The LORD had said to Abram, "Go from your country, your people and your father's household to the land I will show you. I will make you into a great nation, and I will bless you; I will make your name great, and you will be a blessing." (Genesis 12:1–2)

Chapter 11
CREATED FOR PURPOSE

He has saved us and called us to a holy life—
not because of anything we have done but
because of his own purpose and grace.
(2 Timothy 1:9)

IT'S MORE THAN JUST EXISTING

Life for me had been nothing more than a simple existence. I was completely unaware that being in this world meant more than just living one day at a time. The thought of a life goal or some significant contribution to society never crossed my mind. Then one day I heard someone say that life is more than just day-to-day existence. I began to wonder if God had a plan or some significant purpose for my life. Then I came face-to-face with this reality as I turned on the television to hear that we are all created by God with "purpose" in mind.

I tuned in to the programming on the Christian channel and was completely engaged as I heard the minister say, "God has a purpose for each one of us. It is something that we are to accomplish while we spend our time here on earth." I listened intently and found it quite fascinating that God created every person, having purpose for them first. I didn't know if this statement was accurate, but if God had created me with purpose for my life, I was determined to find out what that purpose was.

As this gentleman continued to speak, I heard him say, "Let me put it to you this way: God is everywhere and sees everything, He knows the end of our lives before we ever live our first day. If I can help you arrive at the conclusion of what I'm trying to explain, it is like this." Then he began to demonstrate with his hands.

As he lifted up his right hand with his palm up as if he were holding something in it, he said:

> *God created a purpose, and he holds it in his hand. Then God asked, "Who can I get to fulfill this purpose?" That's the moment that God thought about you and planned to bring you forth to fulfill this purpose. So God began to go to work—bringing your parents together, so they could fall in love, marry, and eventually have you. In time, you faced different challenges while you were growing up and learned a multitude of lessons through these events. The things you have experienced in your life have been used by God to fashion you for the very purpose he has for you. Through the opportunities and challenges you encountered in your childhood, adolescence, and as an adult, you have succeeded and have come all the way to this time. Then, as you go forward in life, the moment comes when you and your purpose collide together.*

I do not recall anything in the program after this statement. I was consumed by the idea that God had an original purpose for me. He had something that I was to do. *What is the purpose that you have for me, God? Why did you create me? God, surely you did not create me and bring me forth from my mother's womb just so I could take up space while I'm here on earth. What am I supposed to do while I'm here? What did you create me for? Show me what I am to do.*

These questions were not answered immediately. For the next year and a half, I spent time in prayer seeking God. Although answers did not come, I did not give up asking for them. Every day and every night, the quest for purpose consumed my thought life as I went through my days carrying out my responsibilities.

CHRISTMAS EVE

While visiting my mother one day in December of 1994, she shared with me that her desire for Christmas was to have all her children and grandchildren around her on Christmas Day. With that in mind, I let my brother and sisters know. We all agreed to gather and spend the night with Mom and Dad on Christmas Eve.

What appeared to be a simple family gathering would later prove to be the orchestration of God bringing about the revelation of his purpose for my life. My siblings began to arrive, and we all took our things to our rooms.

After putting our things away, we came together in the kitchen. As Dad had designed it to be, the kitchen had always been the place of gathering in our house. Mom was elated to have all her children and grandchildren home, and she began handing out new sleepwear to everyone. We went back to our rooms to put the sleepwear away.

As I was headed back to the kitchen, I heard Mom on the phone, saying, "Oh, I'm sad that you won't be able to make it! All the kids are here and I wanted you to be here with us, but I understand." With that, she hung up the phone and told us that Aunt Billie wouldn't be making the trip from Portland, so we could go ahead and start dinner.

After a full day of running around and playing, all the grandchildren were ready to sleep for the night. I helped my daughters get ready for bed, tucked them in, prayed with them, and kissed them goodnight.

My husband decided he would stay with the children until they fell asleep, so I returned to the kitchen.

While laughing with my family as we shared childhood memories, I couldn't help but revisit the minister's words that remained in the corner of my mind. I realized that all these experiences somehow worked together to form the person I had become. After a few hours, I excused myself for bed. Addressing everyone, I said, "Goodnight, you guys." They all turned and said, "No! Stay in here with us!"

"No, I have church in the morning and need to be there by 9:00 a.m." Then I kissed each one and headed for the bedroom.

THE VISION

Once I was in the bedroom, I stood at the door looking at my family as they were sleeping. I began to laugh as I noticed the sleeping arrangements. My family had successfully rolled around, taking up all available space on the bed. *I guess it's the floor for me!* I thought. I grabbed a blanket and put it on the floor at the end of the bed. As I knelt down there, I immediately began to pray. *God, you created me for a purpose; please reveal it to me.*

It had been a year and a half since I heard the minister and began asking God about his original purpose for my life. *God, it is you I seek. It is your purpose that I desire to know. Father, what do you have for me to do? Why have you created me?*

After I asked this question for what seemed to be endless nights—with no answer given—the Lord took me into a vision. I was standing on top of a gigantic pillar of smoke. The width of this pillar was immense. I was standing on its center, and it looked like I was the size of an ant in comparison. There was something very peculiar about the pillar. Although I was standing in the center, I could look straight down to my left. It looked as though I was standing on its edge. As I continued to look down, I saw what looked like a small spot of red. At first I didn't know what I was looking at. Then the vision zoomed in and the red area seemed to increase in size. Without any spoken words, I was made aware that I was looking at hell. It was then that God spoke with a voice that sounded like a thunderous rushing waterfall. He said, "Preach!"

I was instantly shaken from the vision, and it felt like every cell in my body was rattling from the magnitude of God's voice. As soon as I was aware that I was in my room, I stood to my feet and raised both hands. I exclaimed, *Yes, Lord. I will do it!* Then I thought, *Was that really what God had created me for?* I did not want to doubt what I had heard. At the same time, I wanted assurance that I had heard him correctly. I immediately had a conversation with him. *Lord, I don't want to doubt what you have said. In the Bible, I see you granting confirmation to Gideon through the fleece, so I'm asking you—please confirm your word to me.*

After speaking with the Lord, I was compelled to go out to the living room with my family. I stepped out of the bedroom, quietly shut the door, and walked through the hallway and into the dining room. I then heard the front door of the house open and saw my Aunt Billie walk around the corner.

I said to her, "I thought you weren't coming!"

She said, "We weren't going to come, but as soon as I hung up the phone after talking with your mom, I was compelled to pack our bags, get in the car, and drive up. So here we are!" Little did I know that Aunt Billie's arrival was orchestrated by God to confirm his purpose for my life.

Billie headed to the kitchen as I heard someone else come through the front door. Waiting to see who it was, my brother came around the corner. He said, "Vonnie, I want you to meet my boss." As he said that, a man walked around the corner from the front door. My brother put his left arm around my neck and said, "Vonnie, this is Tim, my boss."

I shook Tim's hand as my brother continued speaking. "Tim, I would like to introduce my sister, Yvonne. She's the preacher in this house!" With an elbow jab to my brother's ribs, I said, "Ha, very funny mister!" It wasn't long after that when I returned to my room.

Back in the bedroom, I stood at the side of the bed, raised my hands, and asked, *God, you confirmed your word to Gideon in the Bible. Would you please confirm your word to me?* Instantly God took me into a vision. It seemed as if a movie screen went up replaying the details of meeting Tim. In slow motion, with my brother standing next to me with his arm around my neck, I watched as he pointed to me saying, "She's the preacher in this house."

I began to weep, having missed it the first time. God graciously confirmed it a second time. With my hands raised and a face full of tears, I declared, *Yes, Lord. I will do it.* Only then did it occur to me that I had no idea how to preach. So with my hands still raised in the air, I asked the Lord to send someone who would teach me. Then I proceeded to give God a list of qualifications for this person. *Lord, it has to be someone who is head over heels in love with you, someone who will be in it for the long haul, and someone who will not give up six months down the road. It has to be someone who's willing to teach me everything that he or she knows about preaching the gospel.*

GOD'S PROVIDENCE

Seven days later, I met a woman at a birthday party. I had seen her at church a few days before when the pastor introduced her and her husband as evangelists who had just returned home from the mission field. I'm not sure how the conversation started, but she began to ask me about myself. For some reason she asked me if I knew what God had for me. I shared with her that God had spoken to me and told me to preach the gospel. I saw this slight grin cross her face as I talked. Then she said, "I'm sorry. I don't mean to interrupt you, but can I ask you a question? What does it mean to you to preach the gospel?"

I smiled back and answered, "I honestly don't know what it means, and I am asking God to help me at this point."

She reached into her bag, took out a stack of envelopes, and handed me one of them. She said, "We are holding a banquet tonight, and I would really like for you to be there." I opened up the envelope to look at the invitation and said, "Thank you very much. I'm honored."

After the birthday party was over, I headed home. I asked my husband if he wanted to go with me to this banquet. He let me know that he had to stay home to prepare for his work week. I decided, then, not to go to the banquet, and I went to my room to rest for a while. When I got up, I looked at the clock and was overwhelmed by a prompting to go to the banquet. I thought, *The banquet is in Bellevue, which is at least a thirty-five-minute drive. I only have twenty minutes before the banquet starts.* Still prompted to go, I prayed, *Lord, help me get there on time.*

This would normally be impossible, but things were not normal in my experiences with God. They were all supernatural, and this evening was no exception.

I quickly got dressed, put on some makeup, brushed my hair, grabbed my coat, and headed for the car. *Lord, please help me to get there and arrive safely.* When I walked into the ballroom, the banquet was just beginning. *Yes, Lord, I made it.* I looked at my watch and was shocked to see that I had gotten ready and had driven a thirty- to thirty-five-minute drive—and only twenty minutes had gone by!

My thoughts quickly changed gears as the hosting MC for the evening's event walked up to the microphone to introduce himself. He then introduced the special guests for the evening, evangelists

John and his wife, Shari. The MC shared a little about their ministry and the work they were doing to share the gospel. Just then a group of men and women entered the room and began serving dinner to those who were in attendance. After dinner, Shari walked up to the microphone and sang a special song for us. Toward the end of the banquet, we were shown a video of the places John and Shari had been. It did not occur to me at this point that John and Shari were preachers of the gospel.

After the video, they asked everybody to pray and ask God what he would have them do for this ministry. I closed my eyes and began to talk to the Lord. *God, do you want me to give? If you want me to partner with them and give financially every month, just give me the amount you would have me commit.* The minute those words came out of my mouth, the Lord said to me, "Offer your services to them."

Astounded by his reply, I quickly opened one eye and looked around. *Uh, Lord, I was asking you about money.*

He said, "And I was asking you for your service."

I instantly thought, *Okay! I will go speak to the woman and share with her what you said.* When I walked up to her, she was surrounded by other women wanting just a moment of her time. I thought, *It's okay. I'll go and speak with her husband and share this with him.* When I approached her husband, he, too, was surrounded by a group of men waiting to speak to him.

I knew they attended the same church as I now did, so I thought I would wait until I saw them later to share what the Lord had said. Ready to head back home, I headed out of the ballroom. Once out, I had to cross a hallway to get to the exit door. When I reached the exterior door and pressed on the crossbar to open it, the next thing I knew I was back in the ballroom walking down the aisle. *How did I get here? I was just leaving the building!*

I noticed Shari walking up the aisle heading straight toward me. She stopped in front of me, and I told her that the Lord spoke to me and told me to offer my services to them. Without a single facial expression, she said, "Okay. We will pray and see what the Lord has to say about it."

I turned and headed back up the aisle, across the hallway, and to the exit door a second time, thinking, *Well—you missed God that time!*

A week later I was standing in the foyer at church. This same man and woman walked in the front door. Shari smiled and asked me if she could talk to me for a moment. "Sure," I replied. We walked over to a bench and sat down. She asked, "What kind of experience do you have?" I knew she was referring to work experience, so I told her that I had not worked since giving birth to my children, but before that I had been a secretary for years.

Immediately after I said this, Shari jumped over me and grabbed her husband by the coat collar. Shaking him, she said, "Did you hear what she said? She was a secretary!" They laughed together, and then she turned to me and shared the story about being out of the country for quite some time. While they were away, the secretary of the ministry suddenly quit. Unfortunately, the office work came to a screeching halt and things in the office were left unattended.

She then asked me, "What hours would you volunteer?" I agreed at that point to volunteer four days a week, working from 9:00 a.m. until 2:00 p.m. This would give me plenty of time to return home before the school bus dropped off my children.

I showed up at the office Monday morning. John walked up the stairs in front of me. Putting the key in the door and unlocking it, he swung the door open and stepped aside to allow me to enter the office, saying, "Welcome to ministry!" As I looked into the office, my very first thought was, *God, what have I gotten myself into?*

Stacks of papers were all over the office floor. I could tell that someone had taken a lot of time to meticulously organize them and bundle them together. It looked like the mail had been accumulating for at least a year. I remember thinking, *Can I do this?* As I took a deep breath, I stepped into my first responsibility. The filing alone would take me several weeks. To my surprise, I did not wonder how this was preparing me to preach the gospel.

Training for ministry was in full swing. As executive secretary, I was exposed to every area of the ministry. At the time, I was unaware of all that I was learning. I simply thought that it was my responsibility to help them succeed, and I wanted to be faithful in serving.

One evening after arriving back home from the office, I was listening to Christian television as I prepared dinner for my family. There was a minister on who was preaching about healing. As I was listening, I began to think back through all the programs I had watched up to this time. I realized that there were different messages that were being preached by different ministers.

Each one of them preached Jesus Christ, but somehow the message each preacher carried was different from the other. Some preached Jesus Christ the healer, some preached a salvation message, and others preached prosperity. It was then that I began my prayer by asking, *God, what is the message that you have called me to carry? Clarify it so that I may be accurate in my declaration. Show me what you desire.*

DELIVERANCE MINISTRY

Immediately I found myself within a dream or a vision that began with the phone ringing. I picked up the telephone and said, "Hello?" The person on the other end of the line replied, "Is Mike there?"

"I'm sorry. You must have the wrong number, there is no Mike here."

She said, "Well, maybe you can help us, We're looking for an exorcist."

I thought, *You're looking for what?*

They continued, "You know, someone who casts demons out of people."

I was confused and even afraid to listen to their request. I quickly hung up the phone. As abruptly as the phone call ended, so did the dream—and I woke up. Instantly, my conversation with the Lord began. *Was this simply a dream? Is this really what the Lord is calling me to? How will this be a message to carry?*

With a bit of apprehension, I asked the Lord for confirmation. *Lord, if this is really what you are calling me to, there would be evidence of it in the Bible.* Not in arrogance, but with genuine concern, I said, *Lord, I have read the Bible cover to cover a few times over. I do not recall seeing the word* exorcist *or reading anything about it. How could this be true if it is not in your Word?*

Suddenly I was compelled to reach for my Bible. As I prayed, I flipped the Bible open. To my utter amazement, it opened to Acts 19:13 (NASB): "But also some of the Jewish exorcists, who went from place to place, attempted to name over those who had evil spirits the name of the Lord Jesus, saying, 'I adjure you by Jesus whom Paul preaches.'"

Stunned, I sat there considering if this was truly the direction that I was to go. I didn't know anything about this topic, except from one of Hollywood's movies that I had seen as a teenager. The thought of what happened in that movie was terrifying! I thought, *I'm afraid to do that!*

As the next few weeks went by, I occasionally thought about the dream, only to be reminded of a dream that I had when I was about six years old. I was down inside what appeared to be a medieval dungeon. As I was standing at one end of a very long hallway in this dungeon, I thought, *I don't want to walk down this hallway.* The lighting in the corridor was an eerie purplish-blue hue, leaving shadows peering on the walls. I looked at the round iron circles that decorated the wall of the corridor. I realized that there were iron bars between each circle that made up the doors to each cell. As I walked, I noticed that these cell doors lined each side of the hallway from one end to the other, with approximately a foot and a half between each iron-rod door.

Suddenly and to my horror, an arm reached out through the bars on my right and grabbed hold of my right sleeve, pulling me until my shoulder hit the bars. To my surprise, the width of the hallway seemed to decrease as another arm appeared through the cell bars on the left side of the corridor, grabbing hold of my left arm. I struggled to break loose from their grips and get to the other end of the corridor. With each step, I saw one arm after another come out from behind every iron-rod door. Each arm grabbed me, pulling on my arms like a tug-of-war, desperate in their desire to be freed from their cells.

I experienced so much fear that the thought of walking to the other end of the corridor overwhelmed me. I crouched down to the floor, placing my hands over my ears, and said in utter terror, "I don't want to be here!" With those words, I immediately awoke from this childhood dream.

As I remembered that dream, it seemed as if I was right back in that dungeon being pulled by people who desperately wanted to be released from their prison. My heart was pounding in fear. I wondered, *Could this be real?* I contemplated the dreams, trying to make some sense out of them.

Then one day in June I was attending a women's meeting at my church. After the pastor shared her message, she asked if anyone needed prayer for anything. She invited the women who needed prayer to come and stand at the front of the church so she could lay hands on them and pray for them.

I had often asked God if he saw anything that might be hindering my walk with him. This day was no different. I closed my eyes and asked, *God, is there anything I might need from you that I'm unaware of? Is there anything that might be hindering what you desire to do in me?* With my eyes closed, I immediately saw myself back in the hallway of that dungeon crouched down on the floor, saying, "I don't want to be here."

Frantic, I opened my eyes and thought, *Why is this dream in front of me again?* Gasping to catch my breath with my heart feeling like it was pounding out of my chest, I got out of my seat, walked to the front of the church, and kneeled down at the altar with the other women. Once I was there, I thought, *What do I need prayer for? Why did I get up and come forward?*

As I took the time to ask myself those questions, the pastor was making her way through the lineup of women and was praying for the lady next to me. Then the pastor stepped behind me and began to pray in the Spirit in another tongue. As gently as she placed her hands on my shoulders, she took her hands off. I thought she was through praying for me as she headed to my right where the next woman was standing, only to catch me by surprise as she kneeled next to me and began whispering in my ear.

She began to tell me that God had been showing me many things in the night hours. I was shocked as she began to tell me about the dream of the dungeon. *How could she possibly know this?* The pastor suddenly seemed to fade away while she was speaking the words. All I could hear was the voice of God: "I have called you! Continue to yield yourself to me, and I will pour out my Spirit and set the captives free. Just know that it shall surely come to pass." I began to weep, knowing that God had spoken yet again! There is no way the pastor could have known any of this, because I always kept my experiences to myself. It became frightfully evident that this was the direction that God was taking my life.

One morning while sitting in my bedroom, I began to talk with the Lord about the things he'd shown me. I prayed, *Lord, I won't go looking for these people, but if you send them to me, I will help them.* I had no sooner made that statement when my home phone began ringing. It was a friend who was in full-time ministry. She began her conversation by saying, "I'm here with a street kid who is strung out on something. He is manifesting demons, and I need someone who knows something about this to come and help. Do you know of anyone?"

I remained silent for a moment while warring within myself. *Do I go and cast the demon out or do I refer someone else?* After battling fear and losing, I responded, "Yes! I do know someone who can help you, and he is right down the street from where you are." I gave her the pastor's name, hoping that she would take the young man to the pastor and get him the help he needed. Then I hung up.

I now stood in my bedroom, gripped by fear. I did not want to go anywhere near the enemy as his threat of harm flooded my thoughts. What would I do if I were to come face-to-face with someone like this young man who was thrashing around on the ground and screaming as demons tormented him? I wouldn't know what to do for him, and I certainly didn't want any dealings with the devil.

Standing there, I simply stated, *God, I think you have made a mistake. You got the wrong person for this, Lord. I'm not strong enough!* With that said, I left the subject with the Lord and did not speak about it again.

For the next six months, I spent all my time focusing on my love relationship with God. I wanted to know him more and get closer than ever to him.

A CAGE OF BONDAGE

One Saturday toward the end of those six months, I was at home with my husband. We were looking forward to spending a quiet weekend at home. As the evening was approaching, my husband looked at me and asked, "Do you want to watch a movie and pop some popcorn?"

"Sure! That sounds good," I answered. He immediately got up and headed into the kitchen to prepare the popcorn while I went through the movie listings.

I began to feel a stirring inside me. I felt anxious because I didn't know what was happening. The popcorn in the kitchen was no longer popping, and I knew it would be just seconds before my husband would come back into the room. This feeling I had increased in measure. Suddenly, I couldn't sit still. Just as my husband walked into the room and stood in front of the sofa to take his seat, the Lord spoke to me. His tone was firm and urgent as he said, "Go to your room now!" I looked at my husband and then glanced toward the room. Without a word, I got up and headed for the room. As I was leaving, I heard my husband say, "Hey, I thought we were going to watch a movie!" I did not even respond to him because the directive to go to my room was so commanding.

As I entered my room, I shut the door behind me. I didn't even bother to turn the light on. I fell to my knees and called on Jesus, when suddenly a spotlight from heaven turned on. It captured my attention. I then realized it was shining on an iron-barred cage that was sitting in the middle of my room. As I gazed upon it, I realized there was someone standing inside the cage. Then, like a video camera, my focus zoomed in on the person dressed in a dingy tattered white robe that had moth holes eaten in it.

It zoomed in again, and I could see a black blindfold over the man's eyes and shackles on his wrists that were cuffed to the iron cell. With a final zoom, I saw that the door of the cell was unlocked and open. Then the Lord said to me, "Satan has lied to my people for years, and this is where they think they are."

As the Lord spoke, I could hear the heartbreak, love, and longing in his voice. With this revealed truth, my heart broke, thinking that God's heart was longing for these people to know the truth. He wanted me to be the one to go tell them. As I felt the weight of his words, I said, *Yes, Lord. I will do it! I pray that you will anoint me for this and that you will help me as I go.*

I recently read one of the best quotes I have ever seen. It was full of purpose and truth. It has been attributed to Mark Twain and many others: "The two most important days of your life are the day you were born and the day you find out why." I have now experienced both of these days—as I have discovered *why*. This was the beginning of a deliverance ministry for me, just as God intended. It has been my privilege and greatest honor to serve my Master by declaring his truth to his people. Jesus Christ is the Way, the Truth, and the Life (John 14:6).

The amazing height, width, and depth of God's love has impacted my life with immense joy! This joy only increases as I consider that God has the same intense, immeasurable, and unconditional love for all. I know that God, in his love for you, has a magnificently designed purpose for your life. I can only imagine the joy you will experience as you seek God and discover why you were born.

REVEALED TRUTH

As I thought about Christmas Eve and other childhood memories, I was aware for the first time that each event in my life was used by God. Every challenge and every lesson was used to shape me for the original purpose of God for my life. Jeremiah 29:11 says, "'For I know the plans I have for you,' declares the LORD, 'plans to prosper you and not to harm you, plans to give you hope and a future.'"

It is not always easy to see God in the midst of our challenges, and it is even more difficult to see how anything good could possibly come from some of them. Though we may not clearly understand at the moment, God can and will use every challenge to help shape us for his purposes. Each challenge we face and each victory we have plays a significant part in shaping who we are, who we become, and, more importantly—it shapes our confidence and trust in God.

This leads me to think of David. As a shepherd boy, David cared for the sheep. When the lion entered the fold to take one of the sheep, David ran toward the lion as God gave him the strength and courage to kill this predator. When the bear came in, David killed it with his hands. These challenges seem to be irrelevant to David's God-given purpose and plan. However, they were the very things God used to shape David. His battles with the lion and the bear established trust in God. When David remembered the lion and the bear, he had confidence that God was for him and would grant him victory with Goliath. These things shaped David as a warrior. As David fought on the battlefield, God shaped him into a king who would fight for and defend his people.

Moses is another great example of God using circumstances to shape us for his purposes. Moses experienced life-threatening circumstances that seem at first to have no purpose, until we look closely to the internal shaping of a man for a God-created purpose.

Though God did not create the challenges, he used them to shape Moses for his purposes. God began his work, hiding Moses in plain sight of his enemy's daughter. Moses's sister, following to see where Moses landed, asked Pharaoh's daughter, "Should I go and find one of the Hebrew women to nurse the baby for you?" (Exodus 2:7 NLT).

Moses was then placed back with his own mother for the first three to five years of his life. This gave his father and mother time to teach and instruct Moses about the God of Abraham, Isaac, and Jacob. This training shaped Moses with compassion that would move him to stand and defend his Hebrew brethren.

Moses, in defending a Hebrew man, killed an Egyptian, buried him in the sand, and fled for his life because Pharaoh sought to kill him.

God even turned Moses's fleeing to the backside of the desert for his purpose. God used it to bring Moses to the burning bush, where he would have an encounter with the living God of Abraham, Isaac, and Jacob—the God he had heard about. This encounter would begin another series of events that would shape Moses as a bold deliverer purposed by God. Moses would command Pharaoh, "Let my people go!" With each God-given instruction, Moses's obedience brought him closer to his God-given purpose. God used it all for the good of Moses, who was called according to God's purpose. As we think of Moses, let us consider our own experiences and how they could be used by God to shape and prepare us for the purpose he has for us.

KEYS FOR YOUR FREEDOM

- Know that your first created purpose is to love God and to love others.

  He answered, "Love the Lord your God with all your heart and with all your soul and with all your strength and with all your mind"; and, "Love your neighbor as yourself."

  "You have answered correctly," Jesus replied. "Do this and you will live." (Luke 10:27–28)

- Believe that God has a divine plan for your life.

  "For I know the plans I have for you," declares the LORD, "plans to prosper you and not to harm you, plans to give you hope and a future." (Jeremiah 29:11)

- Trust that your experiences can be used to shape you for God's purpose.

  You intended to harm me, but God intended it for good to accomplish what is now being done, the saving of many lives. (Genesis 50:20)

Chapter 12
PREPARATION OF A WARRIOR: PART 1

Praise be to the LORD my Rock,
who trains my hands for war,
my fingers for battle.
(Psalm 144:1 ESV)

BE TOUGH AND FIGHT

When I was a little girl, my father didn't always know how to express his love for me with words, yet I was well aware of his love through his actions. He worked hard to care for me and my siblings. He always desired the best for us, and this drove him to push us to do our best in all things.

I remember one morning seeing that look of love and concern in my father's eyes. I was preparing to enter kindergarten, and he was concerned that he would not be there to protect me. So my father did what he knew best: he taught me to be tough and to be a fighter. He taught me that giving up was never an option.

That morning in the living room, my dad got down on his knees and put his hands up in front of me as he encouraged me to double up my fists and swing as hard as I could to hit them. I remember him saying, "Baby, if someone even looks like they want to hurt you, you hurt them first." I know that statement sounds absurd and it seems preposterous to teach a five-year-old to hurt someone, but it is imperative to understand that this was coming from the heart of a man who loved his daughter. He wanted to ensure that she was safe and protected, even if that meant teaching her to protect herself with her fists.

As an adult, I now know why my father taught me to be a fighter. His own childhood was difficult, to say the least. Growing up under harsh circumstances forced him to find the strength to be tough and tenacious—character traits that I would foster myself. Although my father's methods may not have been right, teaching me to be tough and fight was.

Unfortunately, without the proper guidance and understanding, in my young mind the definition of being tough meant being mean and malicious. After I came to know the Lord, he began to draw attention to this wrong mindset and revealed the need for transformation. It was always in God's plan that I would learn to be tough and fight. However, it was necessary for me to begin with the right definition.

The word *tough* means to be strong enough to withstand adverse conditions, using great determination and effort in the face of difficulty and hardship. God's definition of *tough* is revealed in James 1:2–4: "Consider it pure joy, my brothers and sisters, whenever you face trials of many kinds, because you know that the testing of your faith produces perseverance. Let perseverance finish its work so that you may be mature and complete, not lacking anything." James 1:12 says, "Blessed is the one who perseveres under trial because, having stood the test, that person will receive the crown of life that the Lord has promised to those who love him."

Once I understood the proper definition of *tough*, I was presented with opportunities to change my behavior. Unfortunately, changing my definition to God's definition proved to be a difficult task. Instead of taking advantage of the opportunities I was given to change, I would find myself thinking, *I'm not a doormat. I'm not going to just stand back and let people walk all over me.* Regrettably, these kinds of statements and thinking caused me to be malicious and cruel.

NOT AGAINST FLESH

Frustrated in my failed attempts to change my understanding of toughness and fighting, I questioned the Lord: *Why was I allowed to be taught this way if it was wrong? Why would my dad teach me to be a fighter? If this is not what you want for me, then why did you allow it to be ingrained in me?* I was taken by surprise as the Lord immediately answered my questions. I never would have anticipated his words of clarification as he said, "Your father teaching you to be a fighter was not wrong! How he taught you to fight was incorrect."

Revelation came instantly, and I knew that fighting in and of itself was not wrong. God desired me to be a fighter, but how I approached fighting was incorrect. I understood that my fight was no longer to be in the natural realm with flesh and blood. My fight was to be accomplished in the spirit realm, meaning that I would fight against the unseen enemy of my soul—the devil. "For we wrestle not against flesh and blood, but against principalities, against powers, against the rulers of the darkness of this world, against spiritual wickedness in high places" (Ephesians 6:12 KJV).

Based on this revelation, each fight could be won or lost by the choices I make. For every right choice, godly character increases. Every negative choice holds me to a vicious cycle of remaining the same.

Although difficult, I have come to appreciate the challenges I face, knowing the potential they possess for bringing about transformation and victory.

SEPARATE THE PERSON

The Lord revealed that my fight was not against flesh and blood, but against principalities and powers. He also revealed how to fight successfully. One day at church I was standing in the middle of a crowd talking to a friend. During the course of the conversation, something was said that I found to be highly offensive. After leaving the building, I immediately began to rehearse the offense. *I can't believe she said that to me! Who does she think she is?* This rehearsal of the offense only increased feelings of hostility in my heart. At that point, I was ready to let go of the relationship.

Then the Lord gave me clear instructions:

> Yvonne, you can't win this battle unless you are fighting against the right thing. You must always separate the person from the action. Recognize the spirit that works undercover manipulating human behavior and even speech. Remember, Satan is the accuser of the brethren. You can take authority over the demonic spirit in the midst of the situation. This will keep you from being offended by anyone and will give you the victory.

I will never forget this explanation as the Lord intervened in a moment when offense presented itself. Through God faithfully instructing me and granting me understanding, I had an incredible desire to yield myself fully to God. I desired the fulfillment of his will above my own. I searched out his way, not mine. The process of learning to choose God over self was not and is not easy. I learned these lessons through several seemingly unsuccessful attempts to lay down "self." It is a constant ongoing work. In the midst of the work, I learned it is not flesh and blood that I am fighting. My ability to fight must be done in the right way as I fight against the enemy of my soul—the devil—not people. Remember this truth based upon John 10:10: It is the thief (devil) who comes to kill (your hope), steal (your joy), and destroy (your life), but Jesus Christ has come that you might have life, and have it more abundantly.

One thing is for sure: I have come to know and value the magnitude of God's immense love. It is a love that is relentless in its pursuit of me. It is a love that continuously equips me with revelation of who he is. It is a love that provides victory as I experience God's supernatural transforming power.

THE REAL FIGHT

One Sunday morning on my way home from church, I found myself driving down the road on autopilot. I was thoroughly enjoying the warmth of the sun as it beamed through the windshield and rested on my face. Without a single thought in mind, I was taken by surprise as the Spirit of God said to me, "Yvonne, you are not fighting the devil to defeat him; you only think you are." This statement perplexed me, as I had concluded that the only enemy I was fighting was the devil!

As I continued to ponder this statement, the Lord began to unfold it in front of me. He reminded me that Satan is a liar and is the father of lies. With his schemes, the devil casts his lies (referred to in Ephesians 6:16 NKJV as fiery darts) into my thoughts. My enemy, the devil, comes with temptations of lust, fear, anxiety, and doubt, all in an attempt to get me to succumb to his lies. Although the thoughts are initiated by him, I'm not directly fighting him. Jesus Christ fought that fight and triumphed over him on the cross. My fight becomes one that takes place in my thoughts and in my feelings.

Every temptation presented is an opportunity to choose God and his Word above the enticement to do wrong. I must be ready to cast down imaginations and arguments that go around and around in my mind. At that moment, I must apply God's Word to each thought that does not line up with what God says. Second Corinthians 10:5 (NASB) says to take "every thought captive to the obedience of Christ."

The devil whispers things like:

- You are so unworthy to even talk with God.

- What makes you think God wants to hear from you?

- Remember what you did last night when you lost your temper?

- You didn't even bother to pray today.

- You had better grovel for a few days until you have paid a penance before you even think about trying to enter in before him.

All these statements are nothing more than demonic lies. As long as I go by what I feel, I will succumb to the temptation of thinking that I have to do something before God will accept me.

On the contrary, God has already told me in his Word that I am accepted (Ephesians 1:4–5), I am the apple of his eye (Deuteronomy 32:10), I am his beloved (Song of Solomon 2:16), and he will never leave me nor forsake me (Deuteronomy 31:8). The fight is within the arena of my mind, as I must fight against every lie. Will I believe what God says about me or what the devil says about me?

One day as I was driving down the road, the Lord began a conversation with me by saying, "Yvonne, as you face all these challenges, you are thinking that it is about you figuring out how to stand in faith, but it is not about that. These challenges give you the opportunity to discover who I am in the midst of them and over them."

Instantly, I got a glimpse of the Lord in his majesty as he rules and reigns over every event that I encounter. This left me in awe as I realized that he is sovereign over my life! He is in full control. Though I go through challenges, he is there to empower me! Many times we go through situations and believe that God has somehow forgotten us, yet he made it clear that he will never leave us nor forsake us.

With that one word, I discovered that this lesson was not about defending against the attack of the enemy, but it was about knowing that Jesus has already overcome the world. Now born of his Spirit, I overcome by my faith in him and who he is in the midst of my challenge.

REVEALED TRUTH

God's desire is for his children to obtain an overcoming faith. We must know him as a loving Father and learn to trust him and his Word. Though his love for me was made evident when he appeared in my room, at times I would lose sight of him in the midst of a storm. Doubt would infiltrate my thoughts. I would abandon faith and find myself thinking, *God, where did you go?*

I was tired of being tossed back and forth between faith and doubt. I decided to be intentional and make a conscious effort to overcome doubt. I wanted to be empowered with an overcoming faith. Intentional in growing my faith, I read the Word, meditated on the Word, and believed the Word no matter how I felt. I knew this discipline would allow faith to arise in my heart and empower me with a trusting confidence in God.

One night I had a dream that revealed in words how I might find an overcoming faith. The dream opened and I was preaching, saying, "When you can unify what you think in your mind with what you believe in your heart and with what you say, you will walk in the power of God with overcoming faith!" Immediately I woke up, wondering if this was an accurate statement regarding faith. I pondered this dream as I thought about my faith or the lack of it. It caused me to wonder if it was possible to think in my mind what I don't truly believe in my heart. If I speak contrary to the Word of God, does that mean I don't believe it? Will what I believe in my heart affect what I say? Can it be that each of these elements can work together in unity to establish an overcoming faith?

Desperate for clarity, I began searching the Bible until I read Psalm 139:23–24: "Search me, God, and know my heart; test me and know my anxious thoughts. See if there is any offensive way in me, and lead me in the way everlasting."

David was crying out to God. Search my heart (what I believe), know my thoughts (what I think in my mind), and see if there is any offensive way (my actions) in me. David asked God to see if there is anything in these three places (his heart, mind, and actions) that would be grievous to the Lord. David then asked the Lord to lead him in the way that is everlasting.

I concluded that these elements were working together. I said, *Lord, if I have an accurate understanding of these verses and what I said in the dream, please confirm it again. This has the potential to empower all of us in our faith! If it is true, then we can find a mature unwavering confidence in you that will establish overcoming faith.*

The Lord said, "Go to Ephesians 4:13." Without hesitation, I turned the pages and began to read. The Lord opened my eyes to see the confirmation. Ephesians 4:13 says, "Until we all reach unity in the faith and in the knowledge of the Son of God and become mature, attaining to the whole measure of the fullness of Christ."

When we believe in God's Word above all else, when we unite what we believe in our heart with his Word, and when we unite what we think about in our mind with what we say and the actions we take, it will empower a confidence in God that will establish an overcoming faith.

We must remember that we have an adversary who initiates his plans in an attempt to weaken our faith in God. The Bible says in Ephesians 6:11 to put on the whole armor of God so that we can withstand the wiles of the enemy. The wiles of the enemy are schemes and methods he initiates in our thinking through lies, doubts, fears, and lust. That is why we are given the directive to cast down vain imaginations in 2 Corinthians 10:5. God knows that what we think about will affect what we believe in our hearts, and that will have a direct effect on our behavior.

However, Jesus Christ defeated the devil on the cross when he made a public spectacle of him. Jesus stripped the devil of the power of death, hell, and the grave. Jesus paid the price in full to redeem us from the power of sin and has redeemed our lives from destruction. "He was wounded for our transgressions [rebellion], he was bruised for our iniquities: the chastisement of our peace was upon him; and with his stripes we are healed" (Isaiah 53:5 KJV).

We have been given everything we need to be victorious. Our fight is the "good fight of the faith" (1 Timothy 6:12). With intent, our faith can grow as we read the Word, meditate on the Word, and believe the Word—no matter what we might be feeling in the midst of any storm. This discipline will increase our faith so we can obtain a trusting confidence in God that will empower us with an overcoming faith.

KEYS FOR YOUR FREEDOM

- Know that when you go through challenges, it is important to be tough and find the fight within you. Employ the spiritual weapons you have been given!

  For though we live in the world, we do not wage war as the world does. The weapons we fight with are not the weapons of the world. On the contrary, they have divine power to demolish strongholds. We demolish arguments and every pretension that sets itself up against the knowledge of God, and we take captive every thought to make it obedient to Christ. (2 Corinthians 10:3–5)

- Understand that your fight is not against flesh, but you must fight in the realm of the spirit and wage war against an unseen enemy.

For our struggle is not against flesh and blood, but against the rulers, against the authorities, against the powers of this dark world and against the spiritual forces of evil in the heavenly realms. Therefore put on the full armor of God, so that when the day of evil comes, you may be able to stand your ground, and after you have done everything, to stand. (Ephesians 6:12–13)

- Realize that since you are being prepared as a warrior, you must always remember that your fight is spiritual and is not with people. Separate the person from the act, remembering that Satan is the accuser. This will empower you to fight the right enemy and give you the victory in Christ Jesus.

Now have come the salvation and the power and the kingdom of our God, and the authority of his Messiah. For the accuser of our brothers and sisters, who accuses them before our God day and night, has been hurled down. (Revelation 12:10)

- Recognize the real fight. You are fighting against satanic lies of doubt, fear, and temptations. Your victory is in the activation of pulling down the lies.

For the weapons of our warfare are not carnal but mighty in God for pulling down strongholds, casting down arguments and every high thing that exalts itself against the knowledge of God, bringing every thought into captivity to the obedience of Christ. (2 Corinthians 10:4–5 NJKV)

- Trust God for overcoming faith. Be intentional and take him at his word. It is never about how you feel; it is always about his Word.

Trust in the LORD with all your heart and lean not on your own understanding; in all your ways submit to him, and he will make your paths straight. (Proverbs 3:5–6)

Faith comes by hearing, and hearing by the word of God. (Romans 10:17 NKJV)

Chapter 13
PREPARATION OF A WARRIOR: PART 2

I have given you authority to trample on snakes and scorpions
and to overcome all the power of the enemy;
nothing will harm you.
(Luke 10:19)

IT IS IN THE CROSS

Our warfare does not consist of directly fighting the devil to defeat him; he is already a defeated foe. Colossians 2:13–15 says:

> *When you were dead in your sins and in the uncircumcision of*
> *your flesh, God made you alive with Christ. He forgave us all*
> *our sins, having canceled the charge of our legal indebtedness,*
> *which stood against us and condemned us; he has taken it away,*
> *nailing it to the cross. And having disarmed the powers and*
> *authorities, he made a public spectacle of them, triumphing*
> *over them by the cross.*

All spiritual warfare that we encounter today in life is won through the appropriation of Jesus's victory and his cross. Jesus, who was without sin, paid the full penalty for all sin so that the power of sin might be broken. He has defeated principalities and power so that we can receive forgiveness. He has shed his blood so that we can apply the magnificent accomplishment of the cross. Jesus came for this reason—to destroy the works of the devil.

In a dream, I was standing in the doorway of a room that was positioned in the middle of a massive hallway. I got the impression that I was in a large hotel, as I could see doors to other rooms on both sides of the corridor. The hall seemed to stretch for hundreds of yards to my left, yet I could see a doorway at the end of that corridor. When I turned my head to look to the right, I saw yet another door at the other end of the corridor.

I continued to look to my right as the door at the end of the hallway opened. A red tiger came through the door and began to walk toward me. Standing in the doorway of the entrance to my room, I stood watching this red tiger as it made its journey down the hallway. As it got closer to me, it began to crouch down along the floor. Not wanting to get close to me, it pushed its body up against the wall opposite me. It wanted nothing to do with me.

I continued watching the door to my right at the end of the corridor. It opened again. This time a black leopard came walking through the door. It also crouched down along the floor and pressed its enormous body against the wall opposite me. This "parade" continued in the dream with one breed of large feline after another—until the door opened one last time.

This time it looked like a tiny poodle walked through the door. I noticed that it had something around its head, but I couldn't see what it was while it was so far away from me. The poodle strutted confidently down the center of this expanse of the corridor, unlike the other animals that had pressed themselves against the wall as they got close to me.

As this little creature got closer, I could clearly see that it was a poodle. It had a wig tied around its head, making it look like a lion. As it approached me, it stopped in its tracks. It then turned to face me in a mocking manner and sat down. I stood watching and began to laugh out loud as I considered this ridiculous lion costume it was wearing. Right in the middle of my laugh, it opened its mouth and let out a roar that literally paralyzed me in the dream.

I woke up with my heart pounding, trying to catch my breath as I felt the effects of the fear. Then I heard 1 Peter 5:8 (NKJV): "Be sober, be vigilant; because your adversary the devil walks about like a roaring lion, seeking whom he may devour." It was then that the Lord revealed to me two particular things within this verse.

The first thing is that the devil goes about "like" a roaring lion. Satan is the father of lies, and he even lies about his own stature. He is a defeated enemy! The Bible declares in Colossians 2:15, "And having disarmed the powers and authorities, he made a public spectacle of them, triumphing over them by the cross." Jesus stripped Satan of his authority and defeated the kingdom of darkness. Every evil principality and destructive power was defeated and rendered powerless when Christ defeated them all on the cross. In the accomplishment of his death, burial, and resurrection, Jesus established his kingdom and his authority here on earth. He has given his authority to us as believers and followers of Christ.

The second thing revealed is that the devil seeks whom he "may" devour. This word *may* communicates permissiveness. If we are ignorant of his schemes and do nothing to oppose his lies, Satan will try to attack in an attempt to lead us astray. It is like giving him permission to work against us. However, as believers in Christ Jesus, we have been made the beneficiaries of Jesus's victory on the cross! The very definition of *beneficiary* is one who receives benefits, profits, or advantages. This is good news! The cross of Jesus Christ renders its victory in my life, and the enemy is rendered powerless. This truth is crucial if we are going to profit from our Savior's victory on the cross.

As the Lord gave revelation in his truth, he revealed who and what our enemy really is: a defeated foe! His works have been destroyed by Jesus Christ through his death on the cross and through his burial as he descended into the depth of the earth to take back the keys of hell, death, and the grave. Finally, through his resurrection, we receive newness of life! Our understanding of the accomplished work of Jesus Christ on the cross profits us, and we benefit in the application of his victory in our lives!

AUTHORITY IN CHRIST

All my spiritual warfare training began by learning what had been accomplished and given to me through Jesus's victory. In addition to understanding the cross, I had to learn about the authority Jesus has given me. Matthew 28:18 reveals Jesus's authority like this: "Then Jesus came to them and said, 'All authority in heaven and on earth has been given to me.'" Jesus then takes his authority and empowers us with it, as stated in Luke 10:19: "I have given you authority to trample on snakes and scorpions and to overcome all the power of the enemy; nothing will harm you." To walk in the plan and purpose of God, I knew I needed revelation of this truth. I began to pray, *Lord, give me wisdom to fully comprehend the authority that you have given.*

One night I had a dream that I was walking down what looked like an alley. As I walked halfway down this pathway, I saw three men leaning against the wall of a building. One man was tall and slender, but large. The second man was of a medium size and build. The third man was very small in comparison to the other two. As I stepped in front of them, the small man tried to stop me from proceeding down the alleyway. I told him to get out of my way and let me pass. As I spoke to the small man, the large man stepped forward to intimidate me with his size. I took a step closer to him, demanding that he get out of my way.

He puffed out his chest and asked, "Who's going to make me?" I stepped right up to him and grabbed his chin to make him look at me. When our eyes met, I said, "In the name of Jesus, I command you to get out of my way!" He then moved back to the wall.

Suddenly, a woman came walking down the alley and stopped next to me. She looked at me and said, "Don't be mad; we just want to play with you." Immediately in my dream I said, "What fellowship is there between light and darkness?" Then I woke up.

This was the first time that I received revelation about understanding the authority Christ has given. Through several more lessons, God continued to teach me about authority. After one lesson, I thought I understood the authority teachings, but when the next lesson came, I quickly realized that I didn't have a firm grip on the taught concepts. Then one day while I was watching a movie, the Lord spoke to me in the middle of a scene.

The backdrop of the movie was a kingdom that was governed by its king and queen. The king was out on a mission, and the queen was in the court ruling over the kingdom during the king's absence. Some of the king's guards brought before the queen a man accused of a crime. She stood up before this man and rendered her judgment. The man, having been shown leniency, was escorted out of the court.

Then a man who had been caught planning an attack against the king and his people was brought into the court before the queen. The queen commanded him to divulge the plan and all those involved.

When she had all the information she needed, knowing the heart of the king and the authority she possessed as queen, she charged the accused man with treason and handed out judgment.

As the queen sat on her throne, which was at the right hand of the king's throne, God said to me, "Jesus is seated in power at the right hand of the Father. You are seated together with him, and he has given you authority to reign in this life."

I now understood. I'm in Christ! I sit with him and have come to know his heart for his people. He has entrusted me to take his authority to rule and reign in this life. He has entrusted me to take authority over all the power of the enemy.

Jesus destroyed the works of the devil. He is now the ruling king over Satan! He is the King of Kings! He is the Lord of Lords! As he is seated at the right hand of the Father in heaven, in his physical absence he has given us authority!

THE SWORD AND THE ARMOR

In Ephesians 6:10, Paul admonishes us to "be strong in the Lord and in his mighty power." He also reveals that there is a battle in which we are to be actively engaged. This battle is not a physical one, but it is a spiritual one that requires a spiritual sword and armor. In Ephesians 6, Paul uses the armor of a first-century Roman soldier as a metaphor to help us understand the use and strength of the sword and armor we possess.

In preparing as a warrior, it is crucial that we know our enemy and how he operates. Paul says, "Put on the whole armor of God, that you may be able to stand against the wiles of the devil" (Ephesians 6:11 NKJV). Paul identifies our enemy, the devil, and tells us how he operates against us—with "wiles." To be victorious, we must clearly understand the definition of the word *wiles*. Wiles are "devious or cunning strategies used to manipulate or persuade someone to do what one wants."

This is the battle the enemy wages against us. He comes at us with devious strategic lies, fears, and temptations to manipulate or persuade us to move away from God. Satan's desire is to get us to do what he wants. Now that we understand the wiles of the devil, we know that the battles are initiated with lies, temptations, and fear. In understanding this, we can identify the battlefield. Now we can move forward and equip ourselves with the sword and the armor God has provided for us.

In Ephesians 6:10–18, using the soldier's battle dress as a visual, Paul addresses six parts of the armor. I will explain each part in order to give you a simple understanding of how each piece works for our victory. It is very important to understand that every piece of the armor is filled with purpose and power. I encourage you to study in length this armor that God has provided for us.

In Ephesians 6:14, Paul first declares, "Stand." This word does not mean to just stand in place. In fact, it means much more than that. In Greek, this word means to make a stand, to keep your place, or to make firm and establish. Understanding this, we can observe the admonishment made to make our stand, to keep our place in Christ Jesus, and to be firm and established in Christ.

Next, Paul proceeds to tell us how to make this stand. Paul draws our attention to the belt used in the military dress and associates it with our spiritual armor. Paul says, "Stand therefore, having your loins girt about with truth" (KJV). Paul, understanding the power of God's truth, commissions us to equip ourselves with the knowledge of the truth. Paul understood that God's truth would securely fasten and keep in place all the other parts of our armor.

If I do not know God's truth according to Scripture, I can be defeated and fall when the enemy comes with his lies and temptations. I can also find myself drawn away by the desires of my flesh. However, if I'm established in God's truth, I am equipped to fight against the enemy's lies and enticements as I surround myself with God's Word.

Paul continues in verse 14 by saying, "having put on the breastplate of righteousness" (ESV). A breastplate is used to guard every life-giving internal organ. The spiritual breastplate does the same. Jesus's righteousness becomes our spiritual breastplate that protects us. This breastplate is put in place by the acknowledgment of Jesus's moral excellence, virtue, and integrity. This breastplate of righteousness for us is established in Christ Jesus alone. When we accept Jesus as Lord and Savior, we freely receive and are clothed with his righteousness.

The enemy of our soul, Satan, works to lure us away from God by telling us, "God is holy and cannot look at you because your sin is so bad; you're not really saved! You are unworthy to be saved by a holy God!" It is in these types of battles that we must have the belt of truth in place and know that our righteousness is in Christ alone. When we know this truth, we can declare, "I am the righteousness of God in Christ Jesus!" Now we are empowered by the grace of God to make a stand in his righteousness against our spiritual enemies.

In Ephesians 6:15, Paul reveals the necessity of having our feet ready for battle: "And with your feet fitted with the readiness that comes from the gospel of peace." The Roman soldiers wore shoes that were cleated on the bottom. This would ensure steady footing so they would not slip and fall in the middle of a battle, leading to defeat.

The same is true for us in spiritual battle. Let me give you an example: It is like the time while praying in tongues, the devil came with his lie that I had cursed God, and now I would be condemned to hell. Without remembering God's Word, I momentarily slipped into believing the devil's lie. However, with the truth revealed, I knew I had nothing to fear from God. Understanding this truth "fastened" my feet and kept me from slipping in the middle of this spiritual battle.

The devil is always trying to get us to separate ourselves from God, and he will use whatever lie he can. We must be prepared beforehand and know in our hearts that God's salvation is like cleats on our feet. His salvation protects and steadies our feet, giving peace to our souls.

Next, Paul focuses on the shield of the Roman soldier. The shield was used for protection in battle. The shield was used to deflect the enemy's arrows, rendering them powerless to injure the soldier. In verse 16 (NASB), Paul transitions from past tense to an active present tense. He says, "Taking up the shield of faith." The word *taking* reveals that just knowing God's truth and trusting it is not enough. You must put it into action! We must become active by speaking the Word of Truth and placing trust in that Word as we speak it.

Let me give you an example of how I had to employ my shield and actively use it in a major battle. It began with sharp pains in the top right side of my liver. With every pain, I would hear a whisper in my ear: "Something is wrong." Then a flood of imaginations would come that would create the worst scenarios.

On another day I had another pain in my lower back on the right side. This pain was different and more severe. I ended up in the emergency room where the doctors wanted to do a CT scan (computed tomography scan). An hour later, the doctor came back with the results. He said, "You have a kidney stone the size of an apple seed!" Evidently that's a very large kidney stone. The doctor then said, "However, that is not what concerns me. I'm more concerned about this dark spot on the top right side of your liver!" Immediately I felt my heart sink. He said, "Schedule an appointment with your primary doctor and have a follow-up on this. I immediately called my doctor to get an appointment. I went in the next day, and my doctor said, "I have reviewed your CT scan, and now what we will do is wait five months to see if there is any change. So before you leave, schedule your appointment."

As soon as I walked out of the doctor's office, the enemy shot his arrows (destructive thoughts) into my mind. He would say things like, "It's incurable!" A flood of what-ifs penetrated my thoughts. For five months the battle was fierce, as the devil would try to tell me it was life-threatening. I kept my shield employed and active in the battle as I fought against every lie and every pain by placing my faith in God's Word. I would lay hands over my liver and declare, "By his stripes, liver, you are healed, healthy, whole, and complete in Christ Jesus. The blood of Jesus has delivered you from destruction and has healed you. I command you to function 100 percent efficiently and effectively according to your design and purpose!"

One Sunday morning as I was returning home from church, a very sharp pain shot through the right side of my liver. It was more severe than any pain I had felt before. Instantly I declared, "Liver—you are healed!" As I said this, I saw in the spirit each word printed like a typewriter message coming out of my mouth. Suddenly the words made a sharp turn, coming back toward me. I watched as they entered my liver, right where the pain was. Immediately the pain left, and I have never felt that pain again. I returned to the doctor for my appointment, only to hear what I had already known. I'm healed, and in the doctor's words, "It's nothing!" I left the doctor's office shouting praises to God as he gave me the victory in the battle.

The shield of faith requires us to take action by placing our faith in God. This piece of our armor is empowered through a protecting trust established through God's Word. The enemy sends his arrows and lying words and tries to use our circumstances in an attempt to penetrate our hearts, thoughts, and emotions and steer us away from God. However, we have something greater than his lies. We have the truth of God's Word. When we activate our faith, it will shield us as it deflects the arrows of the enemy.

Finally, Paul says in Ephesians 6:17, "Take the helmet of salvation and the sword of the Spirit, which is the word of God." I asked the Lord, *Why are these two pieces of armor the only ones addressed together in one statement?* Without any answer, I continued to think about the question. The next morning, the Lord spoke to me while I was washing dishes. My mind was wandering through many "what if" kind of thoughts. Suddenly I heard the Lord say, "Don't allow your thinking to go in this direction, for your thoughts are as powerful as your words." I thought, *How can my thoughts be as powerful as my words?*

As I tried to understand, the Lord spoke again: "Study the sword again." I looked at every scriptural reference regarding the sword. I was suddenly compelled to get on my knees, and I began to pray in tongues. While praying in tongues, I had a deep inward understanding that I was praying about the sword and the helmet. I laid my hand on my head, and God instantly gave me the revelation regarding my thoughts.

The day before, he had said, "Your thoughts are as powerful as your words." I now understood that my thoughts have the power to influence what comes forth from my mouth. Therefore, it is imperative that my thoughts remain in God's truth. I understood the helmet to be a protecting piece of armor that protects and keeps my soul at peace as my thoughts are fastened to the hope of salvation. This is why the helmet and the sword are listed together. The effectiveness of our helmet rests in our ability to think correctly. We must think according to the knowledge of God's truth and the hope of salvation. In addition, the effectiveness and power of our sword is established in our ability to speak forth God's truth. When we comprehend the power God has given us in each piece of our armor and use them correctly, we can obtain the victory in Christ Jesus in spiritual battles.

I will never forget the night I found the necessity for the offensive and defensive uses of my armor. It was during a casual conversation with my husband when something had been misunderstood and a disagreement began. It did not take long before the disagreement was completely out of control. Instead of allowing it to continue, I said, "I don't want to argue, so I'm going to step out for a bit. I will return later."

I left the house and went for a drive. Crying as I drove, I began to consider the disagreement. Where did it all go wrong? I began to review all the things that were said. Then the Lord said to me, "Yvonne, don't let those words hurt you."

With that statement, he opened up a vision in front of me. I saw two daggers attached to a twelve-inch chain, one dagger on each end. Suddenly, without seeing any hands, I saw the chain and daggers being picked up. They began to spin in circles at each end of the chain. The speed increased as they were spinning around. Suddenly I saw a suit of armor in the vision. As the daggers were spinning, they moved closer to the shoulder of the armor until they made contact. I could hear the clang of the armor as the daggers hit it.

With each strike of a dagger, a spark would fly off the armor's shoulder piece and the Lord would say, "Don't let it hurt you." I knew instinctively that the operative word was "let." I had a choice to make! Would I continue to meditate on the words spoken in a moment of frustration, giving the devil opportunity to use them against me to inflict pain in my heart, or would I refuse to meditate on the painful words and begin to speak God's Word into the atmosphere of my home?

As I continued driving, the Lord opened the eyes of my understanding to see how the enemy works against us if we are not employing the armor God has given us. The Lord taught me that this armor and this sword is to be used both defensively and offensively. Defensively, the armor shields me from injury as I choose to walk in obedience to the Lord. The sword is used offensively as I speak the truth of God's Word into the atmosphere that brings about the change needed for victory.

Let me give you an inside look at how the Lord led me in this battle and revealed the scheme of the enemy. The Lord showed me how a demonic spirit was working against us to bring division. He instructed me to take an offensive stance and take authority over a spirit of strife, conflict, and division. I immediately sprang into action with the Word of God, saying, "I bind the spirit of strife, conflict, and division in the name of Jesus. I take authority over you and cast you out of my house! You can't work against us, and you will not cause us to be divided or angry with each other. I now release the peace of God into the atmosphere of my home. I command a calm to manifest in my home, and I declare that we will be unified!" With that said, I headed back home.

I walked in to find my husband calm and lying down. After I lay down next to him, he rolled over, quickly wrapped his arms around me, and said, "I'm sorry." At that moment, the Word of God cut through all the strife. The peace of God brought healing to our relationship and unity prevailed. Victory can be ours in every challenge if we learn to use our spiritual weapons offensively and defensively.

Hebrews 4:12 says, "For the word of God is alive and active. Sharper than any double-edged sword." It is a life-giving spirit that heals and has power to cut through the lies, tricks, and traps of the enemy.

As I was learning about the power of the sword of the Spirit, the Lord took me into a dream. I was standing in an exterior concrete corridor that was lined with arches similar to those of a castle. I noticed an old friend walk past me. He didn't notice me, so I followed him down a walkway, calling his name. As I continued to follow, I saw him step through a doorway at the end of another walkway. Approaching the door, I stepped into the room. It was a massive white room with gigantic pillars. Suddenly, from behind one of the pillars, a man poked his head out to look around. When he didn't see anyone present but me, he stepped out from his hiding place. I instinctively knew this man was evil. As he came toward me, I noticed another man step out from behind another pillar. Without warning, thirty to forty men stepped out from behind the other pillars.

They all began to charge at me at the same time. Instantly I had a massive sword in my hand. Fighting to defend myself, I plunged the sword into the first man to stop him from attacking me. When the edge of the sword pierced him, he burst with an internal explosion and turned into dust. Now the others were running quickly toward me to try to overtake me. I kept swinging the sword with smooth unbroken swings as I transitioned from one fighting stance to another. These men kept coming at me from all directions.

In this dream, I was using the sword with pinpoint precision, as if I had been a ninja warrior my whole life. As the men continued to rush toward me, they began to charge faster than I could swing. It was then that I awoke from another heart-pounding moment that brought revelation. The Lord revealed that the attackers were not human, they were demons. My sword was the Word of God. When it is utilized in battle, it will annihilate the enemy's attacks, ensuring the victory in Christ Jesus and his cross in our lives. Though challenges will come, we can have peace knowing that God has given us the weapons necessary to win.

REVEALED TRUTH

In John 16:33, Jesus said, "I have told you these things, so that in me you may have peace. In this world you will have trouble. But take heart! I have overcome the world." With every challenge you face, I pray that you will use the opportunity to your advantage. Allow yourself to be trained in knowledge and in the use of the truth of God's Word. Become proficient with the spiritual sword and the spiritual armor God has given you.

KEYS FOR YOUR FREEDOM

- Believe that your victory is in the cross! All warfare is won on the basis of the cross of Jesus Christ and on the shedding of his blood.

  And having disarmed the powers and authorities, he made a public spectacle of them, triumphing over them by the cross. (Colossians 2:15)

- Trust in the authority that Jesus Christ has given you. Be effective in warfare, understanding and using your authority.

  Behold, I give unto you power to tread on serpents and scorpions, and over all the power of the enemy: and nothing shall by any means hurt you. (Luke 10:19 KJV)

- Employ the sword and the armor. There is an active spiritual battle going on, and you are to engage in it. This battle is spiritual and requires spiritual weapons. Every piece of your armor is filled with purpose and power.

  For the word of God is alive and active. Sharper than any double-edged sword, it penetrates even to dividing soul and spirit, joints and marrow; it judges the thoughts and attitudes of the heart. (Hebrews 4:12)

Therefore put on the full armor of God, so that when the day of evil comes, you may be able to stand your ground, and after you have done everything, to stand. Stand firm then, with the belt of truth buckled around your waist, with the breastplate of righteousness in place, and with your feet fitted with the readiness that comes from the gospel of peace. In addition to all this, take up the shield of faith, with which you can extinguish all the flaming arrows of the evil one. Take the helmet of salvation and the sword of the Spirit, which is the word of God. (Ephesians 6:13–17)

Chapter 14
WINNING IN WARFARE: PART 1

But in that coming day no weapon turned
against you will succeed. You will silence
every voice raised up to accuse you.
(Isaiah 54:17 NLT)

THE LORD IS MY REFUGE

One morning as I was spending time with the Lord, I heard part of a familiar Bible verse in my mind: "For He shall give His angels charge over you" (Psalm 91:11 NKJV). After hearing this, I went to the Bible and read all of Psalm 91. I moved quickly through the words. My focus was on the fact that God had given his angels charge over me. Focused on the angels, I stopped and said, *Thank you, Lord!* I was surprised when he quickly said, "You missed it. Read it again."

I picked up the Bible and began to read the chapter again. This time I focused on "the snare of the fowler" (Psalm 91:3 NKJV). I knew this was referring to the devil, who lays traps trying to ensnare us. With my attention on this portion of the chapter, I said, *Lord, I know this!* He replied, "No, you don't! You didn't see it! Read it again." A bit frustrated, I picked up my Bible again. I decided I would read the entire chapter very slowly. Finally, I saw it in its entirety.

As I read the first verse, I was overwhelmed at my position in Christ Jesus: "He who dwells in the secret place of the Most High." I had never really given much thought to this portion of Scripture. The Lord asked me, "Where is the secret place?" I was not really sure, until the Lord asked, "What is a secret?"

A secret is something that is hidden, I responded. Immediately the Holy Spirit brought Colossians 3:3 to my remembrance: "For you died, and your life is hidden with Christ in God." I said, "That's the secret place! It's in Christ Jesus! And with my life hidden with Christ, I abide under the shadow of the Almighty!"

That is why I can say with confidence "He is my refuge and my fortress; my God, in Him I will trust," just as it reads in Psalm 91:2 NKJV. Having already identified from verse 3 the fowler as the devil and his snares as the traps he sets, I took note of verse 4: "He shall cover you with His feathers, and under His wings you shall take refuge." I thought about the way a baby chick runs when it senses danger. It fully trusts that it can run and hide under its mother's wings for protection.

Immediately the Holy Spirit reminded me of Luke 13:34, where Jesus said, "Jerusalem, Jerusalem, . . . how often I have longed to gather your children together, as a hen gathers her chicks under her wings, and you were not willing."

The Lord led the way as he asked me, "Do I have feathers and wings to cover you?" He created me and knew I would go study the words to learn their Hebrew meanings. I quickly retrieved my study books and looked up the different words. It's amazing to see the graphic picture the Bible paints for us, so we can see the Lord in action on our behalf.

The word *cover* in Hebrew means "to hedge in, to block, and to overshadow." The word *wings* in Hebrew means "to put into a corner, to be cornered, to be hidden." Let me share the deeper meaning of this verse as the Lord shared it with me. He opened my eyes to see that when the enemy sets his traps against us, we have our lives hidden with Christ. We can run to God in trust, and he covers us. He corners us, meaning that he places us safely in a corner and stands in front of us to block the enemy's attack.

This makes me think of a sheepfold in Israel. The sheepfold is an enclosure that provides protection against thieves and robbers. John 10:10 says, "The thief [the devil] comes only to steal and kill and destroy." The sheepfold also provides protection from the wolves. After the shepherd brought his flock in to keep them safe, he would lie down in front of the door. Nothing could get through that door without having to climb over the shepherd first. Even if the wolves could be heard outside the sheepfold, the sheep remained quiet and at peace in the presence of their shepherd. This is exactly the same picture that Psalm 91 portrays for us. Jesus is our Good Shepherd, our Protector, and he corners us and stands in front of us (at the door) to block the enemy. This is why Psalm 91:5–6 (NKJV) says, "You shall not be afraid of the terror by night, nor of the arrow that flies by day, nor of the pestilence that walks in darkness, nor of the destruction that lays waste at noonday."

As I read verses 9–14, the Lord pointed out that he said "because" three times. He shared with me that his promises in these verses are a blessing for those who are saved: "Yvonne, *because* you have made the Lord your dwelling place, no evil shall befall you." For the first time, I saw his promise of divinely protected health and well-being. As I considered his promise, I was overwhelmed by his goodness, grace, unfailing love, and his faithfulness to watch over me. I know I can confidently place my trust in him. I can cast my cares upon him, knowing he cares for me (1 Peter 5:7). I can lay down my fears, knowing he is with me.

Psalm 91:14–16 (NKJV) says, "Because he has set his love upon Me, therefore I will deliver him; I will set him on high, because he has known My name. He shall call upon Me, and I will answer him; I will be with him in trouble; I will deliver him and honor him. With long life I will satisfy him, and show him My salvation."

As the Lord led me through the last three verses of Psalm 91, he highlighted every statement that began with the word "because." Putting it all together, he shared:

> Yvonne, because you have made me your dwelling place, giving your life to me, your life is now hidden with Christ. Because you have set your love upon me and you love me with all your heart, soul, mind, and strength, and because you have known my name—the power of my name, my authority, my nature to care for you, and my character as a loving Father— Yvonne, you can call upon me and I will answer you. I will be with you in trouble, and I will deliver you and honor you. I will satisfy you with long life and show you my salvation.

I'm grateful the Lord brought correction, wisdom, and revelation to me as he directed me to read Psalm 91 three times. Reading the Bible is a lot like eating natural food. Reading too quickly to get through the Bible is like taking a big bite of food and swallowing it whole. There is not much benefit to it because my body cannot absorb many of the nutrients out of that bite. In like manner, my soul does not absorb nutrients from God's Word when it's read quickly. If I read the Bible and just consider what I read on the surface, I will absorb some life-giving nutrients, but I will not receive the full benefit of it. It's like taking a smaller bite but not chewing it long enough. I chewed, but still didn't receive *all* the nutrients. However, if I read the Bible and take time to study what I have read, the full benefit of the Word of God is released into my life as I absorb it into my heart. From that point, the Word fuels a spiritual metabolism and vitality to act.

Just as I finished reading Psalm 91, a severe pain shot through the upper part of my abdomen. I instantly placed my hands over it, speaking this word: "By his stripes, I am healed. I take authority over sickness in the name of Jesus." After this prayer, I thanked the Lord for showing me Psalm 91, and I thanked him for his promise of protecting my health.

REVEALED TRUTH

God is a loving and faithful Father. He desires to keep us safe from impending danger. In John 16:13 we read, "But when he, the Spirit of truth, comes, he will guide you into all the truth. He will not speak on his own; he will speak only what he hears, and he will tell you what is yet to come." The Lord desires to watch over you, and if you will listen, he will give you the instruction you need to remain safe, just as he did for me that day.

We can see how God gives instruction to keep us safe as we read in Matthew 2:13 NLT, "After the wise men were gone, an angel of the Lord appeared to Joseph in a dream. 'Get up! Flee to Egypt with the child and his mother,' the angel said. 'Stay there until I tell you to return, because Herod is going to search for the child to kill him.'"

As we make the Lord our dwelling place and abide under his shadow, God reveals that we have nothing to fear. He will watch over us, keep us, and protect us according to his truth.

KEYS FOR YOUR FREEDOM

- Remember, *because* you made the Lord Jesus Christ your dwelling place, the promise of divine health and well-being are given to you, and God will satisfy you with long life.

"Because he loves me," says the LORD, "I will rescue him; I will protect him, for he acknowledges my name. He will call on me and I will answer him; I will be with him in trouble, I will deliver him and honor him. With long life I will satisfy him and show him my salvation." (Psalm 91:14–16)

- Trust that if you have not made Jesus your Lord and Savior, you can do it right now—and you will be saved. This simply means to confess that you have done wrong and ask him to forgive and save you, and he will answer.

  If we confess our sins, he is faithful and just to forgive us our sins, and to cleanse us from all unrighteousness. (1 John 1:9 KJV)

  Everyone who calls on the name of the Lord will be saved. (Romans 10:13)

- Trust that God is a refuge from the storm and a shelter from danger. You can confidently place your trust in him, knowing that his love for you is sure and he will make a way.

  Whoever dwells in the shelter of the Most High will rest in the shadow of the Almighty. . . . No harm will overtake you, no disaster will come near your tent. (Psalm 91:1, 10)

- Trust that God will always lead you into victory when you are in Christ Jesus. Jesus triumphed over sin and death, just as he triumphed over Satan and his demons. He conquered every challenge and every temptation. He conquered hell, death, and the grave so that you could be led in his victorious triumph.

  But thanks be to God, who always leads us in triumph in Christ. (2 Corinthians 2:14 NASB)

- Know that being a believer and follower of Christ Jesus does not mean that you are exempt from encountering trials. However, you have been promised that your trials will not overtake you. No weapon formed against you will prosper.

I have told you these things, so that in me you may have peace. In this world you will have trouble. But take heart! I have overcome the world. (John 16:33)

No weapon that is formed against you will prosper. (Isaiah 54:17 NASB)

Chapter 15
WINNING IN WARFARE: PART 2

For whatever is born of God overcomes the
world. And this is the victory that has
overcome the world—our faith.
(1 John 5:4 NKJV)

CALLING 911

Another sharp pain hit my abdomen, and I continued to speak the Word regarding healing over my body as I got up off the floor. I walked out into the living room as my daughter was getting ready to leave for work. I walked over to the picture window to open the blinds, and another pain shot through me.

My daughter looked at me with concern on her face. "Mom, do you want me to stay with you? I can call in to work and let them know that I need to stay with you."

"No! That's okay, baby. You go to work. I'll be okay," I replied. After I assured her that I was okay, she left for work. About five minutes later, another pain punched my abdomen. This one was so bad that it dropped me to the floor. I immediately thought, *I'm in trouble! I need to get to the phone and call someone.* The phone was on the other side of the room. I couldn't move to pick myself up off the floor. With each attempt to cross the room, the pain got worse, until it felt like it was piercing right through me.

To this day, I still do not know how I made it across the room to the phone. I picked the phone up and called a friend who was just minutes away. I told her something was very wrong and that I needed to get to the hospital. I asked if she would come and take me. It felt like only seconds had gone by before my friend was at my front door.

She helped me get to my feet and tried to walk me out to her car. I opened the car door and raised my leg to step into the car, only to have another piercing stab render me breathless. At that point, I must have given her a look that let her know I was in serious trouble. She said, "I'm calling 911."

Making my way back into the house, my friend helped me onto the sofa in the living room and quickly dialed 911. It was not long before I had a houseful of emergency workers. They started by pulling out a machine and attaching monitors to my chest. I told them, "It is not my heart."

When the tests for my heart registered normal, they decided to move me into the ambulance and take me to the hospital. One of the emergency medical technicians went out to the ambulance to get the gurney. As they attempted to place me on it, I was screaming, as the slightest movement sent me reeling in excruciating pain.

FACING DEATH A SECOND TIME

The EMT said, "I'm going to contact the doctor on call in the emergency room to see if we can get permission to give her morphine in order to transport her. With this pain, we can't take her anywhere right now." He stepped outside on the front step to contact the emergency room doctor. He quickly walked back into the house and said that his walkie-talkie was dead and that he needed to use his partner's.

His partner handed his walkie-talkie to him. The EMT again stepped outside to contact the emergency room.

He came back inside and said, "Your walkie-talkie is not working either. I'm going out to the ambulance to use the phone." He came back just seconds later and said, "I don't know what is going on. The phone in the ambulance is not working either. We have no way to contact the doctor to get permission to administer the morphine."

As he stood there perplexed, he said to his partner, "I'm going to give her the morphine anyway. There is no way we can transport her without it. She is in too much pain!" They agreed on that decision. The EMT then pulled out a syringe, placed the needle into the bottle, and drew the morphine. I watched as he stuck the needle into my upper right arm by the triceps and injected the morphine. Then they headed for the ambulance, lifting me in as quickly as they could.

Lying there on the gurney, I felt the morphine travel like fire up my arm, increasing in strength as it began to feel like a forest fire. It reached the top of my shoulder and went up the back of my neck. When it reached the base of my skull, it exploded! It felt as if a firebomb had gone off inside my head as the explosion forced the fire around to the front of my face.

I began to shake my head, for it felt like a flamethrower was being held to my face. The EMT noticed the shaking and asked, "Mrs. Grant, are you okay?"

"No!" I exclaimed. "Something is terribly wrong!" I knew instantly that I was going to be physically sick. Immediately, both EMTs were rushing around attaching me to equipment inside the ambulance. They wrapped the blood pressure cuff around my arm and began pumping it up.

It was then, as both EMTs focused their attention on stabilizing me, that I fully realized I was dying. I literally felt my spirit exiting my body through my feet. I was completely aware that my spirit was halfway in my body and halfway out. I was instantly gripped by a fear greater than any I had ever experienced, as thoughts of dying and of my children and my husband went through my mind. I began to feel incredibly weak physically until I was no longer aware of my body.

CONQUERING FEAR

I was increasingly aware of my combat with fear as I was unmistakably facing death. My spirit departing from my physical body left me growing weaker. With each shallow breath I felt hopeless, as fear clouded out every other thought. I was no longer concerned or aware of anything but the fear of death. As a Christian, I would have thought that there would be nothing to fear in death. I was assured of my eternal place since Christ Jesus was my Savior and Lord, but shockingly, I was not thinking about this truth.

I'm unsure of how or even why, but suddenly, as I faced the fear of death, I was reminded of Psalm 91. "Wait a minute!" I shouted out loud. It just occurred to me that what I had read that morning said that God would divinely protect me. Upon this revelation, I shouted, *God, you are the one who created me. You are the one who gives me life, and nothing or no one takes it away unless you permit it to be so. God, I trust you!* Instantly, I felt my spirit return to my body, strength manifested as I became aware of my physical body again.

Completely taken off guard by my outburst, both emergency workers collected themselves and began to speak to each other in medical terms. I'm not exactly sure how I understood what they were talking about since I had absolutely no medical training, but nonetheless, I knew. The lead technician was giving direction to administer a second medication that would counteract the effect of the morphine.

With the second injection, the burning began to subside as the technician took my blood pressure again. When he finished reading the numbers, he said, "Mrs. Grant, your blood pressure is dangerously low. We need to tip the gurney upside down to get the blood back up to your heart. They turned me upside down to aid in the blood flow. Shortly after this, they closed the ambulance doors and drove to the hospital. Upon our arrival, the doctor met us at the emergency doors. After being administered a barrage of medications to counteract the morphine, my blood pressure stabilized and I began to feel better.

After several hours in the hospital, I was released to my family so they could take me home. On the way home, I rehearsed every memory of God's power and deliverance in my life. With one memory after another, gratitude to God poured out of me: *Lord Jesus, thank you! You have been so faithful. You have strategically broken the chains that held me in captivity. You have annihilated the power of darkness from my life. You have broken the chains of addiction and delivered me from the bonds of depression. Now you have broken the power of death for me a second time.*

REVEALED TRUTH

In the Bible from Genesis to Revelation, we find the heart of God toward man. From the foundations of the earth, God's love had already initiated a plan to redeem fallen man and reconcile us back to himself. His love made every provision for us as Jesus hung on the cross and declared in John 19:30, "It is finished."

God set this plan into motion that we might receive mercy, grace, and the forgiveness of sin. When we understand and believe that Jesus Christ, the Son of God, came and paid the penalty of sin, which was death, in order to reconcile us to God, we believe unto righteousness. When we accept his sacrifice, death on the cross, and confess our sin to him, we receive his salvation. Our spirit is then born again, and we become a new creation in Christ Jesus.

We then receive the Spirit of Christ and must learn how to live our lives with him. The success of our new life with Christ begins with a deliberate forgetting of the life we once lived without him. We must renounce (abandon) that old life with its sin.

As we surrender to Christ, giving up our will to embrace his, we will experience an incredible freedom. This freedom does not mean we continue to do whatever we want. May we always remember the chaotic outcome of life when we did it our way. I know by experience that a life of submission to God can give us a joy that surpasses understanding. It can hold us in a place of peace and comfort that we have never known before. This does not mean that we will never encounter challenges again, because we will. However, we will have a Savior who will walk with us and keep us as we walk with him.

KEYS FOR YOUR FREEDOM

- Believe God's love is here for you. It is unfailing, unfaltering, and unending. It is everlasting, and it will give you peace.

  The Lord appeared to him from afar, saying, "I have loved you with an everlasting love; therefore I have drawn you with lovingkindness." (Jeremiah 31:3 NASB)

- Know that if you find yourself bound and feeling hopeless, you can find hope in God.

  Israel, put your hope in the LORD, for with the LORD is unfailing love and with him is full redemption. (Psalm 130:7)

- Trust in Jesus to take away your sin, and you can become the righteousness of God in Christ.

  God made him who had no sin to be sin for us, so that in him we might become the righteousness of God. (2 Corinthians 5:21)

- Understand that God never intended for you to walk through life trying to change yourself. This is the very reason God provided for you a helper, the Holy Spirit.

  But I tell you the truth, it is to your advantage that I go away; for if I do not go away, the Helper will not come to you; but if I go, I will send Him to you. (John 16:7 NASB)

- Know that the ability to hear the voice of God is one of the greatest gifts you have been given as a child of God.

  Call unto me, and I will answer thee, and show thee great and mighty things, which thou knowest not. (Jeremiah 33:3 KJV)

- Know that yielding to God is the process of denying yourself — your wants, your will—taking up his will, and following Christ.

  Then said Jesus unto his disciples, If any man will come after me, let him deny himself, and take up his cross, and follow me. (Matthew 16:24 KJV)

- Know that you have been created on purpose, for purpose!

  Your eyes saw my unformed body; all the days ordained for me were written in your book before one of them came to be. (Psalm 139:16)

  For we are God's handiwork, created in Christ Jesus to do good works, which God prepared in advance for us to do. (Ephesians 2:10)

Chapter 16
CONCLUSION

So there I was, in the midst of my misery, wanting to escape a life of lying, cheating, stealing, and addiction—when Jesus Christ appeared. In kindness and with genuine love, Jesus responded to the deep cry of my heart with one question: "What are you going to do?" The choice I made transformed my life. During the process of my journey, I learned that there are spiritual keys available to us that can unlock the provision of heaven and empower us to walk in freedom in Christ Jesus.

Transformation in every area of life always begins with a choice. We can continue doing things our way, or we can surrender to the Lord—who is the Way, the Truth, and the Life. I now fully understand that Jesus Christ is the number-one key for transformation, and our supernatural journey to freedom begins there.

When I finally accepted a life with Jesus, he sent his Spirit to abide in me. His Spirit became a guiding presence who continues to lead me in freedom every day. This does not exclude me from experiencing other trials or suffering through hardships, but it empowers me to endure and be victorious in them. A major key to success in walking with the Lord has been learning to be congruent with him. It is his power that keeps me in freedom as I walk out my spiritual life being obedient to his leading.

Only by hearing God's voice can I respond to him in obedience. This was crucial as I learned that my adversary, the devil, would try to keep me in obscurity. Satan would impart his lie, trying to convince me that I could not hear God's voice. That was far from the truth, and Jesus himself said, "My sheep hear my voice." I simply had to learn to recognize it and make sure it lined up with the Bible, because God will never contradict what is written within its pages.

As I read the Bible, I came to know God, his character, and his nature toward me. Though I met a loving, patient, kind, and forgiving God, my thoughts would get twisted up in the lies of my adversary, and I would begin to view God through my natural understanding, thinking he was angry when I made mistakes.

I discovered that faith was the key to the kingdom of God. Faith has the power to unlock the provision of heaven, and knowing this truth made me free to walk boldly with him.

Intimacy with Jesus daily reminds me how much he loves me. Every time I stop to spend time with him, more passion is produced. It is in his presence that I find everything I need, including love, faith, courage, and hope. This reality has become the key that empowers me to keep moving forward in good times and in trying times.

However, in each trying time I must choose to surrender. No matter the scenario, I must be willing to humble myself before God and acknowledge my motives and actions. In yielding to God, I have learned to take responsibility for the things I say and do. This causes me to grow in my relationship with him and with others.

As long as we remember that God is in control and we can trust him with our future, we can move forward, lean back, and rest in him. Let us keep in mind that resting in God does not mean we sit back and wait for him to do everything. We must be active in applying the keys that are given and fight the good fight of faith. Our fight is waged with the Word of God. It has the power to deliver us and set us free from any addiction. It has the power to bring us out of depression. It has the power to sear right through fear or anything else that would try to keep us from a full relationship with Jesus Christ.

If you have never surrendered your life to Jesus, you can do it right now. Just pray this prayer: *Lord Jesus, I come confessing that I need you. Forgive me of my sin, wash me, and cleanse me from all unrighteousness. Be my Lord and Savior. Baptize me with your Holy Spirit with the evidence of tongues, and I will yield my life to you as you empower me to live it. In Jesus's name I pray. Amen.*

Now you can begin your supernatural journey with Christ to freedom and be transformed using the keys that have been provided.

****

Lord, you are creator of all, a faithful loving Father, a constant transforming presence, and an ever-present abiding help. As I look back and remember all that you have done to set me free and transform my life, I'm overwhelmed by your grace. You carried me through every challenge, every trial, and every hardship. You have transformed me from the inside out. You have empowered me with strength and have given me victory in the battles. I love you so much. I'm forever grateful and forever yours.

Order Information

CPSIA information can be obtained
at www.ICGtesting.com
Printed in the USA
LVHW032308300419
616204LV00001B/166